$ W9-BVL-207

4/27/86

Presenting
READER'S THEATER
Plays and Poems to Read Aloud

OTHER BOOKS BY

Caroline Feller Bauer

HANDBOOK FOR STORYTELLERS

MY MOM TRAVELS A LOT

THIS WAY TO BOOKS

TOO MANY BOOKS!

CELEBRATIONS

A RAINY DAY

A SNOWY DAY

Presenting
READER'S THEATER

Plays and Poems to Read Aloud

by Caroline Feller Bauer

DRAWINGS BY
LYNN GATES BREDESON

THE
H. W. WILSON COMPANY
1987

Library of Congress Cataloging-in-Publication Data

Bauer, Caroline Feller.
  Presenting reader's theater.

  1. Drama in education. 2. Children's plays.
3. Reader's theater—Study and teaching (Elementary)
4. Language arts. I. Title.
PN3171.B37   1987   792'.0226   87-2105
ISBN 0-8242-0748-3

Printed in the United States of America
First Printing

ACKNOWLEDGMENTS

The author is grateful for permission to
include the following works.

"Ali Baba and Princess Farrah" adapted from *The Adventures of Ali Baba Bernstein* by Johanna Hurwitz. Copyright © 1985 by Johanna Hurwitz. Adapted by permission of William Morrow & Company.

"Ant" from *Forgetful Wishing Well* by X. J. Kennedy. Copyright © 1985 by X. J. Kennedy (A Margaret K. McElderry Book). Reprinted with the permission of Atheneum Publishers, Inc.

"At the Airport" adapted from *Switcharound* by Lois Lowry. Copyright © 1985 by Lois Lowry. By permission of Houghton Mifflin Company.

"Beyond Expectations" from *The Phantom Tollbooth* by Norton Juster. Text copyright © 1961 by Norton Juster. Reprinted by permission of Random House, Inc.

"The Bridge over the River Clarinette" by Pierre Gamarra, translated by Paulette Henderson. Reprinted by permission of *Cricket* magazine. Copyright © 1973 by Open Court Publishing Company.

"A Bug Sat in a Silver Flower" from *Dogs & Dragons, Trees & Dreams: A Collection of Poems* by Karla Kuskin. Copyright © 1975 by Karla Kuskin. Reprinted by permission of Harper & Row, Publishers, Inc.

"Cockroach" by Yoshiko Uchida. Copyright © 1985 by Yoshiko Uchida.

"Colors" from *Yes I Can* by Dennis E. Smith. Copyright © 1986 by Dennis E. Smith. Monterey Road Gang, Publishers (Redlands, California). Reprinted by permission of the author.

"The Common Egret" from *I Am Phoenix: Poems for Two Voices* by Paul Fleischman. Text copyright © 1985 by Paul Fleischman. Reprinted by permission of Harper & Row, Publishers, Inc.

"Dragons and Giants" from *Frog and Toad Together* by Arnold Lobel. Copyright © 1971, 1972 by Arnold Lobel. Reprinted by permission of Harper & Row, Publishers, Inc.

"Fifteen Seconds" from *Mind Your Own Business* by Michael Rosen. Copyright © 1974 by Michael Rosen. Reprinted by permission of Andre Deutsch Ltd.

"The Greedy Man's Week" from *A Bunch of Poems and Verses* by Beatrice Schenk de Regniers. Text copyright © 1977 by Beatrice Schenk de Regniers. Reprinted by permission of Clarion Books/Ticknor & Fields, a Houghton Mifflin Company.

"How the Camel Got His Hump" from *Just So Stories* by Rudyard Kipling. Reprinted by permission of Doubleday & Company, Inc.

"If We Walked on Our Hands" from *Something Special* by Beatrice Schenk de Regniers. Copyright © 1958, 1986 by Beatrice Schenk de Regniers. Reprinted by permission of the author.

"I'm Tipingee, She's Tipingee, We're Tipingee, Too" from *The Magic Orange Tree and Other Haitian Folktales* by Diane Wolkstein. Published by Alfred A. Knopf, Inc., 1978. Reprint edition published by Schocken Books, 1980. Copyright © 1978 by Diane Wolkstein.

"In Which Tigger Comes to the Forest and Has Breakfast" dramatized from *The House at Pooh Corner* by A. A. Milne. Copyright © 1928 by E. P. Dutton & Co., copyright renewal © 1956 by A. A. Milne. By permission of Curtis Brown Ltd., London.

"Jamboree" from *One at a Time* by David McCord. Copyright © 1965, 1966 by David McCord. By permission of Little, Brown and Company.

"Jump Rope Rhyme," copyright © 1983 by Charlie Meehan. From *The Chocolate Book: A Sampler* by Michael Patrick Hearn, copyright © 1983 by Caedmon, New York. Reprinted by permission of the publisher.

"The Knee-High Man" from *The Knee-High Man and Other Tales* by Julius Lester. Copyright © 1972 by Julius Lester. By permission of the author.

"The Land of the Bumbley Boo," from *Silly Verse for Kids* by Spike Milligan, published by Puffin Books. Reprinted by permission.

"Learning" from *If I Were in Charge of the World and Other Worries* by Judith Viorst. Copyright © 1981 Judith Viorst. Reprinted with the permission of Atheneum Publishers, Inc.

"The Library Cheer" by Garrison Keillor. Copyright © 1983 by Garrison Keillor. All rights reserved. Reprinted by permission of the author.

v

For Hilary
The Queen of Hearts
With love,
The M

Thank you to:

Patsy Clark, Niagara Falls, New York

Marsha Cutler, Las Vegas, Nevada

Judie Davie, Greensboro, North Carolina

Art Evidon, Lisbon, Portugal

Susan Guisti, Rabat, Morocco

Alice Hosstetter, Los Angeles, California

Sharon Johnson, Anaheim, California

Harriet McClain, Sitka, Alaska

Joan McLemore, Meadville, Mississippi

Marie Raymond, Sacramento, California

Judy Schoenstein, Princeton, New Jersey

Susan Steele, Dhahran, Saudi Arabia;

and to all my workshop participants from Algeria to Westerville, Ohio, who tried out the plays and offered valuable suggestions at every stage; and to Ellen Lehman, who said no, and yes, and gets four hugs and three kisses.

Contents

Presenting
READER'S THEATER
Plays and Poems to Read Aloud

Introduction

I HATED Margaret O'Brien.

You're too young. You don't even know who she is. Never mind. Just say it was a case of Envy, and you notice I've used a capital *E*. Margaret O'Brien was about my age and she starred in movies when I was in elementary school. I was sure that if I could just be "discovered," I would be much more popular than she was, and certainly a far better actress. O'Brien always appeared sickly and wan, while here I was, bursting with energy and health, standing up straight in the subway just in case a talent scout happened to be on the same train!

I loved acting in plays, and although my reading skills were poor when we had to answer questions or look up vocabulary in class, I especially enjoyed any kind of reading aloud, even when I stumbled over words. At home my parents read plays out loud and I often joined them. In the sixth grade, I wrote a spoof of *Romeo and Juliet* (and played Juliet, of course) in which a popcorn seller planted in the audience disrupts the important balcony scene.

At least in those days classes were small enough to perform plays. Now there are three or four fourth grades in a school, and the staff is expected to find a way to display all the children in the Christmas program. I think there were many more opportunities for students to perform when I was in elementary school than there are today. Beverly Cleary, author of many favorite children's books, recalls an actual class called Assembly in which children were trained to stand up in front of the whole school and recite.

Well, I don't really want to be Margaret O'Brien anymore (how about Barbra Streisand?). But I admit that I love to perform, and I guess that's what I'm doing in the workshops I hold across the country each year. And I love to encourage people to perform with me. That's why I think Reader's Theater is such a wonderful invention. It allows all of us, would-be stars or not, to participate.

Reading is fun! Why must we convince people of this? Perhaps because we put entirely too much emphasis on perfect test scores and top grades. I hope that Reader's Theater will help more children realize that reading can be entertaining, and that it need not always be linked to skill sheets and test questions.

I have written this book to give children a chance to enjoy literature. I've included a variety of classic folktales, selections from contemporary children's books, and poetry, all choices that work particularly well as Reader's Theater plays. I hope teachers, librarians, media specialists, and parents will use this collection to introduce children to the joy of reading through drama.

What Is Reader's Theater?

Reader's Theater is a form of oral presentation with an emphasis on reading aloud rather than on memorization. Since there are no lines to memorize, this is an activity that virtually everyone, including shy children and unsure readers, can participate in. The focus should be on *reading*. Encourage everyone in your group to volunteer for a part.

Although people have distinguished between different forms of Reader's Theater, calling one style Chamber Theater and another Story Theater, I prefer simply to think of this entire method of performance as Reader's Theater.

There are no rules in Reader's Theater. The only requirements are a group of eager participants and a set of scripts. You can add props and stage settings if you like, but the wonderful thing about this kind of performance is that it does not require props, costumes, makeup, or elaborate stage settings. Remember, simplicity is the key.

You may want to create your own scripts. Perhaps you have already written some. I have found, however, that many teachers, librarians, group leaders, and parents simply do not have the time to search for appropriate material and then take still more time to adapt it to play form. Several years ago, when I first became interested in Reader's Theater and began composing my own plays, I thought that if there was a plentiful source of ready-to-use scripts, perhaps Reader's Theater would become a "do it today" activity instead of a "someday" activity.

THE SCRIPTS

I've chosen materials for a variety of tastes and reading levels. For instance, you'll find scripts based on such diverse materials as a favorite chapter from Beverly Cleary's *The Mouse and the Motorcycle*, a French folktale called "The Bridge over the River Clarinette," and a triplet of poems about food.

Since many children are not proficient at reading aloud at their own silent reading level, I've chosen material that most seven- to twelve-year-olds will be able to read. As the director, you will want to read the scripts and decide which are most suitable for your group. The short introduction that precedes each full-length play will help you by indicating the difficulty level of the script and also suggesting the setting and the mood of the play; in effect, it sets the stage for you. These introductions are for you *and* your children. You might wish to read the relevant parts aloud to both the audience and your players, as a preface to your performance. The poems, of course, are not full plays, but they make perfect short presentations. Introduce your children to these writers with fast, fun "poetry breaks." And finally, don't be afraid to use a script several times with the same group. The more often you read a script, the more confident your group will feel with it.

How Do I Use Reader's Theater?

JUST FOR FUN

Perhaps you have a few minutes at the beginning of a language arts class, at the end of a library skills lesson, or in the middle of a book club meeting. Gather a set of scripts and ask, "Anyone want to be in a play?"

Choose the number of upraised hands that equals the number of readers in the play you've chosen. Assign the parts: "Malik, you'll be the narrator," "Lori, you are the frog," etc., pass out scripts to the players, and just let the children begin to read.

Don't criticize. Let your group enjoy reading aloud. Remember that the main object of these scripts is for children to enjoy reading aloud in a nonthreatening environment. Try a poem or even a set of poems (I've grouped some thematically for just this purpose) if you have literally only a few minutes. If you have ten or fifteen minutes to fill, choose a longer play and enjoy the break in routine.

Involving Everybody

We get into a lot of trouble believing that *everyone* must participate in *everything*. The whole class is not on the baseball team. There is no reason why everyone must be in a performance. However, I'm sympathetic to those of you who have 25 children you would like to involve in a Reader's

Theater production. Be creative. You don't have to find a play with 25 speaking parts—use three plays with five parts, four poems with two parts. Have one child introduce each play, and another introduce the poems.

You can involve twice the number of players actually reading parts and also give nonreaders or poor readers a chance to perform by having a group of "actors" accompany the reading with appropriate gestures. Readers can stand next to or sit in front of actors. This is a good way to handle plays with stage directions calling for various actions. Some examples in this book are "Ruby," "I'm Tipingee, She's Tipingee, We're Tipingee, Too," "Down with President Stomach," "Ali Baba and Princess Farrah," and "In Which Tigger Comes to the Forest and Has Breakfast."

Several of these skits ask the audience to repeat a phrase or perform an action. In fact, you should stress to your class that the audience has just as important a role as the players. Spend a few moments working with your audience. Remind the members of the audience that their role is to support the players. An obvious way for an audience to show support is by applauding after each scene. You can have children in the audience practice applauding, so that they will be waiting eagerly for their part at the end of the scene.

WITH A LITTLE PRACTICE:
WORKING TOWARD A PERFORMANCE LEVEL

One day, perhaps not long after you begin tucking Reader's Theater performances into spare moments, someone will suggest giving a play for another class, for some of the parents, or maybe for the principal.

Although I've emphasized the ease and spontaneity of Reader's Theater, most of us love to perform before an audience (even if we never wished to be Margaret O'Brien!). To work one of these script readings up to a satisfactory performance level, you will have to set aside a bit more time than the few minutes that it takes to read aloud informally. You can prepare a more formal presentation at one sitting or meet several times. I've listed some easy steps to a polished performance below.

Silent Reading

Begin by drawing the performing group away from the rest of the class and forming a circle. This will give the group a feeling of intimacy and shared fun. Before you assign parts, each player should silently read through the entire script. Make sure you allow plenty of time for this, so that everyone has a chance to read slowly and carefully. If you have a low-level reading group, you may wish either to read the script aloud or to paraphrase the story before your players read the script to themselves. This way, you can be sure that everyone understands what the play is about.

Round-Robin Read Aloud

Now, still before assigning parts, read the script round-robin style. If your readers are not particularly strong, you can take part as well. Simply begin by asking the player on your left to read the first paragraph, the next person to read the second, and so on. This gives your children a chance to test their "performance" voices and to gain confidence in their speaking ability.

When you have finished reading the script aloud, discuss each of the characters in turn. What do they look like? What defines their personalities? How do they sound? You might even discuss what happened to these characters before the play begins and what might happen to them later, particularly if you've chosen a selection from a full-length book. Spend just as much time discussing a small part as you do a main role. Emphasize that the narrator, the player (or players) who introduces the play, provides narrative detail, and sets the mood of the performance, is also a character. In fact, the narrator must be a strong reader who can guide the play and maintain an appropriate pace.

Finally, review the pronunciation of any words that are troublesome. Do this in a general way, without criticizing any one person's reading.

Casting

The tendency in assigning parts is to give the strongest reader the best part. If the President of the United States (or your mother-in-law) will be attending the presentation, then I don't blame you for wanting to show off your best students. However, since this is supposed to be for fun, why not let everyone play whatever character they want?

Once you have assigned parts, make sure each player has a script and ask the children to highlight their particular speeches. Provide highlighters in several colors and let the children have fun marking their passages; if this isn't feasible, underlining individual parts in pen, pencil, or crayon also works well.

Now read the play through again, but this time each player should read his or her part. Remember to practice with special care those sections where the script calls for "all" players to participate.

When suggesting how to improve a player's intonation, pronunciation,

5

projection, or posture, be sure to refer to the character's name rather than the name of the child playing the part. This softens the criticism, since it distances it from the child.

Rehearsal

Once you've selected your players, assigned parts, and read through the script, you are ready to rehearse. This is best done in the room where you will give your performance. If this is not possible, mark off an area similar to the stage or performance area you will be using.

When directing your players, use actors' stage directions. UPSTAGE is away from the audience. DOWNSTAGE is toward the audience. STAGE LEFT is the actors' left when facing the audience and STAGE RIGHT is the actors' right.

UPSTAGE

STAGE RIGHT   STAGE LEFT

DOWNSTAGE

AUDIENCE

Offstage, arrange your players as listed in the player lineup at the beginning of each script. Ask the players to carry their scripts in the hand farthest away from the audience. The first person in line, usually the narrator, gives a signal and the players walk in and line up downstage in a row or semicircle.

The leader counts orally or by a hand movement and all players bring their scripts to chest height. At another signal, the players open their scripts. The first player begins speaking. As the players introduce themselves, they should take a few steps towards the audience (downstage), and then step back into line. For a smooth performance, the entrance and script handling should be practiced, but as director you must decide if perfecting these movements will detract from your players' enjoyment or add to it, and direct accordingly.

As you will see, there are a few informal stage directions from time to time. We've included these because although this is _Reader's_ Theater, sometimes a line just seems to call out for an accompanying action. For instance, the character Clyde in "Ruby" doesn't speak at all, but he has many actions to perform. In most of the plays, though, the actions are not at all necessary. Direct your group to try them, if you like, or ignore them if you prefer to concentrate on simply reading.

Next, I suggest actually practicing in front of a small audience, perhaps the other half of the reading group or a few students from another class. After the first rehearsal performance, ask your readers to tell you what they thought of their presentation, and make any suggestions you think would be helpful to them.

Speaking Up

The biggest problem children have in performing Reader's Theater is their lack of projection awareness. This may sound unprofessional, but I tell my performers to shout and yell. They sometimes also tend to speak too quickly at first and then compensate by speaking v-e-r-y s-l-o-w-l-y. The best solution to these problems is to make sure your players are very familiar with their lines, so that they can concentrate on speaking well. Again, this is to be a fun activity, not an exercise or lesson. Try to be very positive and frequently compliment your players.

Focus

Since this is Reader's Theater, you will achieve action only through focus. The focus is the person to whom the players address their lines. Since the children are reading from scripts rather than speaking from memory, there is a danger that they may spend the entire play with their heads—and voices—buried in their scripts. I advise a fixed audience focus. The players imagine that a particular spot somewhere in the audience is the person to whom they are speaking. This way, the players speak out into the audience and the audience feels more involved in the play as well. Another option is to have the players direct their speeches to each other by actually turning to face the player reading the character being addressed in the script.

As director, you must make the purpose of focus clear to your players. If they understand the principle, you can say "watch your focus" or "pay attention to the focus" to quickly correct any drift toward mumbled speeches. Players should also be reminded that they must stay in character even when they are not actually reading lines.

Equipment

I'm not really getting fancy, just being practical. After your readers have lost their places in the script and scattered papers all over the floor, you'll understand why professional troupes use music stands. But please, please, don't feel that if you can't find music stands, you can't perform the plays.

If you're in a school with a music department, the obvious place to get stands is from the music teacher. The stands should be placed in the performing area before the players enter. The scripts should still be brought on stage by the performers, so there will be no confusion about whose script is where.

Many performers use music stools along with the stands. The idea is that since music stools rotate, a character can twirl in or out of a scene. When the character is on stage, he faces the audience; when he leaves the action, he rotates a half circle and remains with his back to the audience. I personally don't like to use stools with children. First of all, it's a big bother lugging them about. Secondly, as a performer it's not much fun having your back to the audience during most of the performance. And lastly, just think how much fun it would be for a nine-year-old to spend valuable rehearsal time revolving on her stool!

Folders and Flyers

The illustrated title pages for the scripts in this book, drawn by Lynn Gates Bredeson, make perfect folder covers. Duplicate them along with the scripts and let the children color the designs. Glue the title pages onto plain manila folders and place the pages of the scripts inside.

If your children have trouble keeping the pages of their scripts in order, you may want to staple the pages. This is not as attractive, because the audience will see the scripts when the pages are turned, but it is certainly better than having pages fall to the floor in the middle of the play. Another idea is to staple the scripts into the folders at the top and bottom of the left edge of the script pages. Crease the pages about ¼-inch from the left edge, so the pages will turn smoothly. You can also punch holes in the scripts and folders, tying them together with colorful yarn or string. The advantage of this method is that the folders are then easily reusable.

The script title pages also make perfect promotional flyers. Just write the time and place of your performance on the illustration, copy it on colored sheets of paper, and give to anyone you would like to attend your play. You can also hang them on bulletin boards or leave a stack for visitors to your library or classroom.

Tickets

At the end of each play we have provided a ticket for that play. Duplicate these to give out to audience members or to your players as souvenirs. Point out what great bookmarks they also make!

Finding an Audience

No matter how informal your Reader's Theater program is, it can be fun to have some sort of an audience. When we think of an audience, we may think of the thousands of fans who fill a stadium to listen to a rock star. But, of course, an audience can be as small as one person: a teacher, a librarian, or a school administrator, for example. It can be just a few interested people gathered in the library or classroom after lunch. It can be a sports team or a reading club. For more formal presentations, try performing at a parent open house, in a senior citizens' center, or as part of an after-school program.

Remember, Reader's Theater only works if your children enjoy reading the scripts and are enthusiastic about participating. Don't insist on performing before the entire PTA if your players have more fun reading just for each other.

Warm Ups

When Johanna Hurwitz, a children's book author, begins to write for the day, she does a bit of writing just to warm up. She sits down at her word processor and writes a letter to *me*. (That's how I happen to have twenty years of letters from my friend.) Warm-up exercises are considered a must if you are going to engage in any physical activity. Singers warm up their voices before singing. Track stars warm up before a meet. We can use reading aloud exercises to prepare for a Reader's Theater performance. Use this little group of exercises to warm up voice and mind before you read a play or a set of poems. You can even try an exercise just for fun anytime you need a break in routine.

GIVE AND TAKE READING

Choose a passage from a favorite book and have your group (no more than 20 people) sit in a circle. Then ask each person to begin silently reading the passage. Explain that whenever a player wishes, he or she should say a word or a sentence or two aloud and then fall silent. Only one player at a time may speak. To set the pace, the leader can begin the exercise by reading out loud at a pace that is appropriate for the group.

We usually think of reading as a solitary activity. This exercise is fun because although each person reads silently, the shared phrases draw the members of the group together. With a bit of practice, this exercise can sound quite eerie and mysterious.

READING AND LISTENING

For this exercise each person will need a partner. One person reads a passage silently while the other person relates a recent experience ("what I did last weekend," for example). You should allow four or five minutes for this activity, so that the person reading silently can begin to concentrate. When the leader says stop, the person who was reading must describe not only what she was reading but also what she heard. The partners then switch places, so that the other person can see what it feels like to try to do two things at once. Most people find that they can listen better than they can read. Many students try to do their homework while listening to a television or radio. Are they really reading effectively? Still, this is just for fun, so we don't need to come to any scientific conclusions.

ARROW STORY

This is a listening exercise that requires group participation. Choose a story or try the one below. I've inserted pauses to indicate when the group should join in. You will need a paper arrow large enough for your group to see from a distance. You can make one quickly and easily from poster board. Hold the arrow with the point up to indicate that your group should be silent. Begin telling the story, and pause in the spots I've marked to turn your arrow. As you move the arrow to the side, the group can begin to respond out loud with the appropriate sound effect. By the time the arrow reaches the 6:30 position, the group should be shouting. As your arrow reverses position, the group should respond more softly, until everyone is silent again.

Marcie was sitting alone in the house. Outside she heard the wind howl____. Rain began to fall____. There was a scratching at the door ____. Maybe it was a lion____. Maybe it was a mouse____. Maybe it was a monster____. She was scared. She turned on the radio to drown out the scratching. The radio was playing "Jingle Bells"____. (She turned it low/high/off.) The telephone rang____. She answered it. It was a singing telegram that sang happy birthday to Marcie____. At the door the scratching continued____. She opened the door____. Her dog came in, jumped up, and gave her a big kiss____.

PLAY AN EMOTION

In this exercise each player chooses or is assigned an emotion or characteristic. Then open a discussion topic such as "what flavor ice cream should we serve at the party?" or "how old must you be before you can drive?" Each person must respond to the question "in character," and the group must identify the trait or feeling the person is trying to portray.

Use words from this list, choosing those that will be most appropriate for your children:

angry	enthusiastic	consoling
scared	annoyed	domineering
amused	argumentative	aggressive
restless	pompous	exultant
brave	apologetic	reckless
bored	agreeable	suspicious
sleepy	picky	motherly
tired	sexy	greedy
skeptical	pessimistic	decisive
confused	opportunistic	effervescent
upset	humble	rude
disgusted	nervous	lazy
mean	sly	self-indulgent
crazy	scholarly	obsequious
shy	dictatorial	combatant
excited	slavish	sophisticated
sad	disorderly	macho
impatient	obstreperous	precocious
flirtatious	morose	threatening
dreamy	impertinent	haughty

SILENT BIRTHDAY LINEUP

This is a nonverbal exercise to do if you would like to have your children get up and move around a bit before they begin their work. The directions are simple: Ask your children to line up by the day and month of their birthdays. They may not speak, but they may use hand motions to communicate. When everyone seems to have found his or her place, begin at the head of the line and see if everyone is in the right place by having the children count off by month and day. How close can your group come to forming a perfect line?

NAME AND MOTION, PLEASE

This is really an "ice-breaker," a good activity to introduce a group of strangers to each other. Players form a circle. Each person says his or her name and accompanies it with a distinctive action (jumping, throwing arms in the air, whirling around, etc.). Then ask who can repeat each person's name and action.

CIRCLE STORY

If you have ever gathered around a campfire, you probably have played a variation of this game. Players sit in a circle, and the leader begins a story with "Once upon a time there was. . . ." The next person must continue the story for a sentence or two from that point, then stop for the next person to continue. For instance, if the first person stopped with the word "and," the next person may not say "and" but must continue with the next word. When your group really becomes proficient with this exercise, you can take people out of order to finish the story rather than continuing in a circle, by saying "cut to Ann," or "cut to Ronnie." Imagine how many funny and inventive stories your group can create!

This same idea can be used as a writing exercise. A player writes a sentence on a sheet of paper, ending with a transitional word such as "and," "but," "or," "however," etc. He or she then folds the paper over so that the sentence is hidden and hands the paper to the next person, who writes a sentence, folds the paper over, and so on. The last person may write a concluding sentence and then stand up and read the entire story aloud.

Here are some more exercises to stretch your imagination, your body, and your voice:

MIME

Individual Exercises

Pick up a glass.
Open a door.
Put on a coat.
Jump rope and miss.

Walk on a tightrope over a pit filled with tigers.
Walk home after a party through dark, empty streets.
Wait for the results of an important test to be posted.
Try to fall asleep when sleep won't come.
You are five years old and eating popcorn while watching a movie.
Take a stubborn dog for a walk.
Try to read while a bee buzzes nearby.
Wait for a bus in a rainstorm without an umbrella.

Remain completely silent and listen first to your own body (breath, heartbeat), then to the sounds within the room (a light buzzing), finally to exterior sounds (rain, cars, birds). Allow at least five minutes of silence to experience this exercise.

Recreate a Moment

Show how your emotions differ when you are:

listening to a symphony	attending a church service
enjoying a rock concert	watching a football game

Change

Put up a real or imaginary sheet and change from:

elephant to mouse	angel to witch
princess to football player	old man to young boy
preacher to clown	frog to prince
policeman to crook	

Reactions

Show your reaction to winning a:

lollipop	frog	car	million dollars

VOICE EXERCISES

Partner Skits

Someone cuts into the cafeteria line; the other person is annoyed.
A child begs her mom to let her go to the circus.
Give a good excuse for missing your piano lesson.
Two children enter a haunted house. One is brave, the other is fearful.
Explain to the principal why you put a lizard in the librarian's purse.

Imitations

Imitate:

a cuckoo	an elevator	a cat stranded on a roof
a lawnmower	a train whistle	a scolding parrot
an airplane	a wind storm	a hungry baby

CHANTS

Group chants make good warm-up exercises because they give players an opportunity to use their voices together. In these chants the leader usually

recites the verse and the group responds with the chorus. After the children
have heard the chant a few times, they may join in from the beginning.

A Peanut Butter Sandwich Chant
(Fa-Mi-Re)

CHORUS: Peanut, Peanut Butter, Jelly
Peanut, Peanut Butter, Jelly

First you take the peanuts and you smash 'em, you smash 'em
First you take the peanuts and you smash 'em, you smash 'em

CHORUS: Peanut, Peanut Butter, Jelly
Peanut, Peanut Butter, Jelly

Then you take the grapes and you squish 'em, squish 'em
Then you take the grapes and you squish 'em, squish 'em

CHORUS: Peanut, Peanut Butter, Jelly
Peanut, Peanut Butter, Jelly

Then you take the bread and spread it, spread it
Then you take the bread and spread it, spread it

CHORUS: Peanut, Peanut Butter, Jelly
Peanut, Peanut Butter, Jelly

Then you take the sandwich and you eat it, eat it
Then you take the sandwich and you eat it, eat it

Start singing Peanut, Peanut Butter, but with your mouth
closed because the peanut butter is making it sticky.

Marsha's Song

Five little worms went crawling along
And as they went they sang this song:
It's RRROUGH being a worm
It's RRROUGH as can be
'Cause so many things can happen to me.

Just then a big bird came flying by
He saw the worms and—GASP! Oh my . . .

Four little worms went crawling along

16

And as they went they sang this song:
It's RRROUGH being a worm
It's RRROUGH as can be
'Cause so many things can happen to me.

A boy on a bike went peddling by
He didn't see the worms and—SQUASH! Oh my . . .

Three little worms went crawling along
And as they went they sang this song:
It's RRROUGH being a worm
It's RRROUGH as can be
'Cause so many things can happen to me.

A girl going fishing just came by
She took a worm and we know why

Two little worms went crawling along
And as they went they sang this song:
It's RRROUGH being a worm
It's RRROUGH as can be
'Cause so many things can happen to me.

A hungry chicken came pecking by
She saw the worms and—GULP! Oh my . . .

One little worm went crawling along
And as he went he sang this song:
It's RRROUGH being a worm
It's RRROUGH as can be
'Cause so many things can happen to me.

A girl picking berries came his way—
But this was really his lucky day—
'Cause she went by
And we know why—
Nobody likes worms in berry pie.

My Name Is Sew

Begin chanting and ask your children to join you with words and actions as soon as they catch on to the rhythm.

17

Hi
My name is Sew
and I work in a button factory
I have a wife and two kids,
one day my boss says to me,
"Are you busy, Sew?"
I say, "No."
"Then push this button with your

RIGHT HAND (continue pushing your right hand as you chant again)

Hi
My name is Sew
and I work in a button factory
I have a wife and two kids,
one day my boss says to me,
"Are you busy, Sew?"
I say, "No."
"Then push this button with your

LEFT HAND (continue pushing with both hands as you chant again)

Hi
My name is Sew
and I work in a button factory
I have a wife and two kids,
one day my boss says to me,
"Are you busy, Sew?"
I say, "No."
"Then push this button with your

RIGHT LEG   (continue pushing with both hands and your right leg as
            you chant again)

Hi
My name is Sew
and I work in a button factory
I have a wife and two kids,
one day my boss says to me,
"Are you busy, Sew?"

I say, "No."
"Then push this button with your

    LEFT LEG   (continue pushing with both legs and both hands as you
                   chant again)

Hi
My name is Sew
and I work in a button factory
I have a wife and two kids,
one day my boss says to me,
"Are you busy, Sew?"
I say, "No."
"Then push this button with your

    HEAD   (continue pushing with both hands, both legs, and your head as
              you chant again)

Hi
My name is Sew
and I work in a button factory
I have a wife and two kids,
one day my boss says to me,
"Are you busy, Sew?"
I say, "No."
"Then push this button with your

    TONGUE   (continue pushing with both hands, both legs, your head and
                your tongue as you chant again)

Hi
My name is Sew
and I work in a button factory
I have a wife and two kids,
one day my boss says to me,
"Are you busy, Sew?"
"I say "Yes!"

The Library Cheer

by Garrison Keillor

Where do you go for the poetry?
L-I-B-R-A-R-Y
Where do you go for the history?
L-I-B-R-A-R-Y
Where do you go if you're old and shy?
Where do you go to learn how to fly?
L-I-B-R-A-R-Y
    That's how you spell it,
    Whatcha gonna tell it?
It's been in your town for a hundred years.
Let's give the library three big cheers:
    Hip-hip-hurray!
    Hip-hip-hurray!
    Hip-hip-hurray!

F-R-I-E-N-D-S
Are we gonna be one?
Yes yes yes.
F-R-I-E-N-D-S
Are we gonna be one?
Yes yes yes.
F-R-I-E-N-D-S (of the)
P-U-B-(huh!) L-I-C
L-I-B-R-A-R-Y

L-I-B-R-A-R-Y
L-I-B-R-A-R-Y
L-I-B-R-A-R-Y
    That's how you spell it,
    Now what you going to tell it?
It's been in your town for a hundred years,
So let's give the library three big cheers:
    Hip-hip-hurray!
    Hip-hip-hurray!
    Hip-hip-hurray!
When I say library you say Card,
    Library

Library
I got one today and it wasn't too hard.
    Library
    Library
Big brick building how sweet it looks,
Takes me on in to the land of books.
P-U-B-(-) L-I-C L-I-B-R-A-R-Y
P-U-B-(-) L-I-C L-I-B-R-A-R-Y
P-U-B-(-) L-I-C L-I-B-R-A-R-Y

SONGS

These three engaging songs, from Dennis E. Smith's collection *Yes, I Can*, make wonderful warm-up exercises.

Yes, I Can

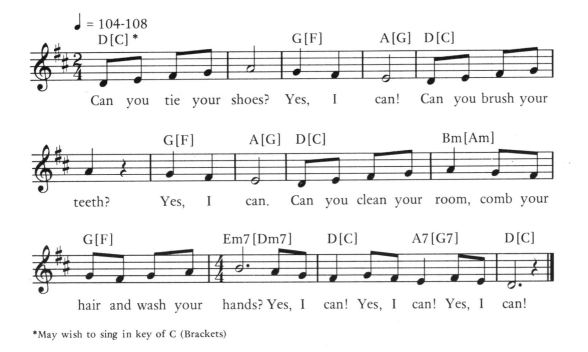

*May wish to sing in key of C (Brackets)

Max the Fly

1. Me, oh, my. ___ Max the fly. He is walk-ing on the ceil-ing,
2. Wish that I were Max the fly. I'd be walk-ing on the ceil-ing,
3. Me, oh, my. I think I spy. Oh, dear Max is on the but-ter,

he is walk-ing on the walls. He is buzz-ing in the kitch-en,
I'd be walk-ing on the walls. I'd be buzz-ing in the kitch-en,
on the bread and sal-ad too. Oh, dear Max, its rude to spoil our

He is buzz-ing down the halls.
I'd be buzz-ing down the halls. } Buzz, buzz, buzz, buzz, buzzzzz.
food; now what are we to do?

(repeat 3 times)

Buzz, buzz, buzz, buzz, buzzzzz. (4.) Think I spy Max the fly. He is

(softly)

walk-ing on the ta-ble ov-er by my Dad-dy's hat. Now to

ritardando - - - - - - -

(loud)

quick-ly grab the pa-per [WHACK!] I think I squashed him flat! Yuk!

(optional)

22

Colors

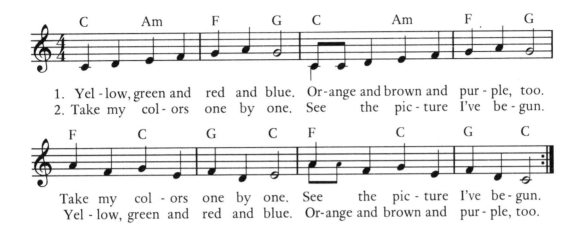

1. Yel - low, green and red and blue. Or-ange and brown and pur - ple, too.
2. Take my col - ors one by one. See the pic - ture I've be - gun.

Take my col - ors one by one. See the pic - ture I've be - gun.
Yel - low, green and red and blue. Or-ange and brown and pur - ple, too.

Zena and Zach and the Sack of Gold

ZENA AND ZACH AND THE SACK OF GOLD

"Zena and Zach and the Sack of Gold" is a story about a farmer named Zach and his wife, Zena. Zena, who loves to gossip, can't keep a secret at all. Zach, who loves Zena, is quite aware of this. In our play, Zach succeeds in fooling the landowner by first fooling his wife.

This is an especially good choice for a large group or class, since the audience has an important part to play as the chorus of forest spirits.

Players: 8+

Narrator 1	Zena, his wife	Townsperson 2
Narrator 2	Townsperson 1	Townsperson 3
Zach, the farmer		Landowner

Audience Participants

NARRATOR 1: I am _____.
    I am a narrator.

NARRATOR 2: I am _____.
    I am also a narrator.

ZACH: I am _____.
    I play Zach.

ZENA: I am _____.
    I play Zena.

TOWNSPERSON 1: I am _____.
    I play a townsperson.

TOWNSPERSON 2:   I am _____.
        I also play a townsperson.

TOWNSPERSON 3:   I am _____.
        I too play a townsperson.

LANDOWNER: I am _____.
        I play the landowner.

NARRATOR 1:   Welcome to our production of "Zena and Zach and the Sack of Gold." You, the audience, will have an important part in this story. You will play the forest spirits. Please practice making the sound of a sheep. (Baa . . .). Good, but we will need to hear it louder. Try again. (Baa . . .). Listen for your cue. When you hear it, you must make your sheep sound. Please try again. (Baa . . .). Thank you.

NARRATOR 2:   There was once a farmer . . .

NARRATOR 1:   Who had a wife . . .

NARRATOR 2:   Who loved to gossip.

ZENA: Did you hear about Karen's cow, Bessie? She's sick.

TOWNSPERSON 1:   (gossiping to townsperson 2) Did you hear about Bessie's cow, Karen? She's had a calf.

TOWNSPERSON 2:   (gossiping to townsperson 3) Did you hear about Karen's calf? She's got 2 calves and one of them is sick.

TOWNSPERSON 3:   (gossiping to townsperson 1) Did you hear about Zena's cow? Her cow Karen has a sick calf.

27

NARRATOR 1:   One day Zach was in the forest when he looked behind a tree and saw,

ZACH: A treasure! A big bag of gold! I'll take it home. No, I'd better leave it here.

NARRATOR 1:   Zach was afraid that his wife, who loved to gossip, would tell everyone that he had found a bag of gold in the forest.

ZACH: Hello, Wife. I have something to tell you, but you must keep it a secret.

ZENA: Of course. I'm good at keeping secrets.

ZACH: I have found a bag of gold in the forest today. Now don't tell anyone!

ZENA: My Zach found a bag of gold in the woods.

TOWNSPERSON 1:   Zena's Zach found a bag of gold in the meadows.

TOWNSPERSON 2:   A lot of gold was found in the forest near the meadow by Zena.

TOWNSPERSON 3:   Zena and Zach are rich.

NARRATOR 2:   The gossip about Zach's discovery reached the landowner. He commanded Zach to appear before him.

LANDOWNER: You can tell me exactly where you found a bag of gold that your wife says you discovered in my forest.

ZACH: I haven't found anything, sir. My wife is always telling strange tales.

LANDOWNER: Bring her here tomorrow. She can tell her own story.

NARRATOR 1:   That night Zach came home late.

ZACH: Wife. Wife. Fry me some pancakes. Lots of pancakes. I'm hungry.

ZENA: This is a strange time to eat, but as you wish.

NARRATOR 1:   Zena made piles and piles of pancakes.

ZACH: These are very good. I'll have more, please.

NARRATOR 1:   While Zena made more and more pancakes, Zach hid some in a knapsack.

ZACH: That's enough pancakes for tonight. Let's go to bed.

ZENA: Goodnight, Husband.

ZACH: Goodnight, Wife.

NARRATOR 2:   The next morning Zach woke up very early.

ZACH: Good morning, Wife. I'm going out now to check my hunting and fishing traps.

NARRATOR 2:   Zach made the rounds of his traps. First, he went to the river and looked at his fishing net.

ZACH: Oh, wonderful. Here is a nice fat fish.

NARRATOR 2:   Next Zach looked in his animal trap in the forest.

ZACH: Oh, wonderful. Here is a nice fat hare.

NARRATOR 2: Then, Zach put the fish in the animal trap and he went back to the river to put the hare in the fish net.

ZACH: There. That's a good day's work.

NARRATOR 2: On the way home, Zach took the pancakes he had stored from his knapsack and put them in the branches of all the trees.

ZACH: Hello, Wife. We are going to find the treasure now.

ZENA: We're going to get our gold today.

TOWNSPERSON 1: Did you hear that the treasure is to be found today?

TOWNSPERSON 2: Zena is going to ask Zach to go with her to find a treasure.

TOWNSPERSON 3: What treasure?

NARRATOR 1: Zach and Zena walked along the path. Zena kept looking up at the trees.

ZENA: Look, Husband. There are pancakes growing in the trees.

NARRATOR 1: Zach took Zena to look at his animal trap.

ZACH: Look. There is something in the trap.

ZENA: A fish is caught in the trap in the forest. That is strange.

NARRATOR 1: Zach put the fish in his knapsack.

30

ZACH: Let us see if there is anything in the fish net.

ZENA: Look. There is something in the net. It's a hare. That is strange. A hare in the river and a fish in the forest.

NARRATOR 2: At last Zach came to the tree that hid the treasure.

ZACH: Here is the treasure. Help me carry it home, Wife.

NARRATOR 2: In front of the landowner's house a group of sheep were grazing.

NARRATOR 1: (motion to audience to join you) Baa Baa Baa

ZENA: What is that?

ZACH: Those are forest spirits. Run home! We must escape them!

NARRATOR 1: (motion to audience to join you) Baa Baa Baa

NARRATOR 2: As soon as Zena and Zach got home, they counted the gold in the sack.

ZACH: This is a lot of gold, Wife.

ZENA: We are rich, Husband.

TOWNSPERSON 1: Zena has lots of gold.

TOWNSPERSON 2: Zach has lots of gold.

TOWNSPERSON 3: Zach and Zena are rich.

NARRATOR 1: That evening Zach took Zena to the landowner's house.

LANDOWNER: I hear you found gold in the forest. Everyone is talking about it. They heard it from your wife, Zena.

ZACH: Oh no, sir. My wife is a bit strange.

LANDOWNER: Zena. Did you and your husband find gold in the forest?

ZENA: Yes, sir.

LANDOWNER: Tell me about it.

ZENA: Well, first we walked on the path where the pancakes are growing in the trees.

LANDOWNER: Pancakes?

ZENA: Then we took the fish out of the animal trap.

LANDOWNER: A fish?

ZENA: Then we took the hare out of the fish net.

LANDOWNER: A hare?

ZENA: And then we found the gold.

LANDOWNER: Ah ha. The gold.

ZENA: And then we heard the forest spirits near your house and ran home.

LANDOWNER: Forest spirits?

ZACH: I told you, sir, that my wife tells a strange story.

NARRATOR 1:   The landowner shook his head.

LANDOWNER: You'd better take your wife home. She needs a long rest. She's seeing and hearing things.

NARRATOR 1:   Zach took Zena home where they used the gold to live comfortably ever after.

NARRATOR 2:   The townspeople are still gossiping about it.

TOWNSPERSON 1:   They found a fish.

TOWNSPERSON 2:   They found a hare.

TOWNSPERSON 3:   They found gold.

NARRATOR 2:   On a clear night you can still hear the forest spirits calling.

NARRATOR 1:   (motion to audience to join you) Baa! Baa! Baa!

NARRATOR 2:   The End.

ADMIT ONE
ZENA AND ZACH
AND THE SACK OF GOLD
Gold

Using Subtraction

By Allan Jacobs and Leland Jacobs

Readers: 2

READER 1: "Using Subtraction"

READER 2: I've often heard the teacher say,
"subtract means less, or *take away*."
And so I'd get great satisfaction
if I could only do subtraction
on all of these—yes, all of these:

READER 1: Liver,

READER 2: spinach,

READER 1: "Quiet, please."

READER 2: scoldings,

READER 1: early bedtime,

READER 2: rice,

READER 1: rainy Sundays,

READER 2: "Do be nice."

READER 1: tattletales.

READER 2: big pills to take,

READER 1: sleet, and smog,

READER 2: and stomachache.

READER 1: Since these all drive me to distraction
for them I'd always
use subtraction.

The Swineherd

BY HANS CHRISTIAN ANDERSEN

THE SWINEHERD

Hans Christian Andersen was a Danish author who lived more than 150 years ago. His stories have been told to generations of children and his work has been translated into many languages. You may know some of his most popular tales, such as "The Little Fir Tree," "The Steadfast Tin Soldier," "The Little Match Girl," and "The Tinderbox." "The Swineherd," also a favorite, tells the story of a flighty princess who is courted and then rejected by a prince because of her selfishness and greed. It is not a somber tale, however. Much of it is very funny and it should be played with a light spirit. You might wish to practice some of the foreign phrases with your group before you begin.

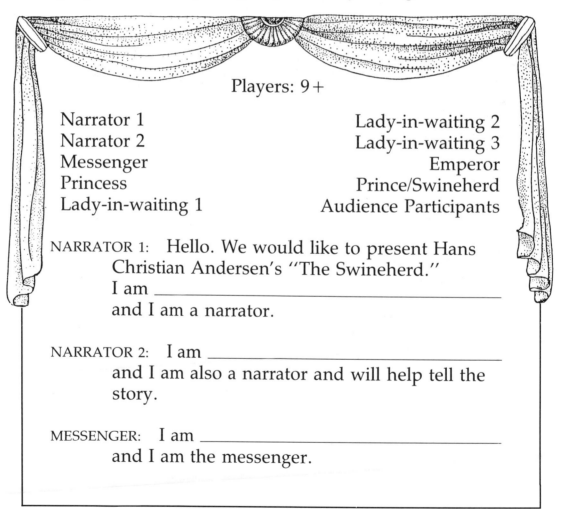

Players: 9+

Narrator 1   Lady-in-waiting 2
Narrator 2   Lady-in-waiting 3
Messenger   Emperor
Princess   Prince/Swineherd
Lady-in-waiting 1   Audience Participants

NARRATOR 1:   Hello. We would like to present Hans Christian Andersen's "The Swineherd." I am _____ and I am a narrator.

NARRATOR 2:   I am _____ and I am also a narrator and will help tell the story.

MESSENGER: I am _____ and I am the messenger.

36

PRINCESS: I am _____
  and I am the princess, the emperor's daughter.

LADY-IN-WAITING 1: I am _____
  and I am one of the princess's ladies-in-waiting.

LADY-IN-WAITING 2: I am _____
  and I am also a lady-in-waiting.

LADY-IN-WAITING 3: I am _____
  and I too play a lady-in-waiting.

EMPEROR: I am _____
  and I am the emperor.

PRINCE: I am _____
  and I play the prince turned swineherd.

Scene One

NARRATOR 1: There was once a poor prince. He had but a small kingdom, but it was big enough to allow him to marry. And marry he would.

NARRATOR 2: Still, it was bold of him to ask the emperor's daughter. He did ask her, though, for after all there were many princesses who would have been delighted to marry such a handsome prince.

NARRATOR 1: And so this is what he did.

NARRATOR 2: A rose bush grew on the grave of the prince's father. It bloomed only once every five years and then only with a single blossom. But what a rose that was. If you smelled it just once you forgot all your troubles.

NARRATOR 1:   He also had a nightingale which sang every lovely melody in the world. The rose and the nightingale were to be presents for the princess. They were put into silver caskets and sent to her.

NARRATOR 2:   The gifts were sent to the great hall where the princess was playing at "visiting" with her ladies-in-waiting.

MESSENGER: I have brought you presents from the prince.

PRINCESS: (clapping hands with excitement) Oh how lovely. I do hope it is a pussy cat.

MESSENGER: It's a rose.

LADY-IN-WAITING 1:   How pretty.

LADY-IN-WAITING 2:   How delicate.

LADY-IN-WAITING 3:   How nicely it is made.

EMPEROR: It is more than beautiful, it is exquisite.

PRINCESS: (reaching out to touch the rose) Fie, Papa! It is not made. It is a real one.

LADY-IN-WAITING 1:   It is real.

LADY-IN-WAITING 2:   It is real.

LADY-IN-WAITING 3:   It is real.

EMPEROR: Let us see what is in the other casket before we get angry.

NARRATOR 1:   The nightingale flew out. It sang so beautifully no one could think of anything to say against it.

LADY-IN-WAITING 1:   Superbe!

LADY-IN-WAITING 2:   Charmant!

LADY-IN-WAITING 3:   Très bien.

NARRATOR 2:   All the ladies-in-waiting spoke a bit of French. All spoke quite poorly.

LADY-IN-WAITING 1:   How that bird reminds me of our late emperor's music box!

LADY-IN-WAITING 2:   Ah, yes. They are the same tunes.

LADY-IN-WAITING 3:   And the same sweet singing.

EMPEROR: You are right. It sings just like the music box.

PRINCESS: It certainly couldn't be a real bird.

MESSENGER: But it is real, Your Highness. It's a real nightingale.

PRINCESS: (stamping feet) Well then, let it fly away. I will not see the prince.

NARRATOR 1:   But the prince was not to be denied. He stained his face and wore his cap low over his eyes.

PRINCE: (knocking) Hello, Emperor. Good morning. Do you have a job I might do here at the castle?

EMPEROR: Well, there are many who wish to work here. But let me think. Yes. I do need someone to look after the pigs. We have so many of them.

NARRATOR 2: So there was the prince. He was made imperial swineherd and was given a horrid little room near the pigsty.

NARRATOR 1: The prince was not idle. He worked all day fashioning a little cooking pot. It had bells all around it and when it was boiling the bells tinkled and sang an old song.

NARRATORS 1 AND 2: (begin singing and motion to audience to join in)

AUDIENCE: Ach du lieber Augustin
Alles ist weg, weg, weg!

NARRATOR 2: But the best part of the cooking pot was that by holding a finger in the steam one could immediately smell all the dinners that were being cooked in town.

NARRATOR 1: That's a very different matter than a rose.

NARRATOR 2: The princess came walking by the pigsty with all her ladies-in-waiting.

NARRATOR 1: The pot began to sound its tune.

NARRATORS 1 AND 2: (motion to audience to sing and help them to start)

AUDIENCE: Ach du lieber Augustin
            Alles ist weg, weg, weg!

PRINCESS: (clap hands) Oh, I can play that tune on the piano.

NARRATOR 1:   (speaking to the audience as though telling them a secret) It was her only tune. She could only play it with one finger.

PRINCESS: This must be a very cultivated swineherd. First Lady-in-waiting, go and ask him how much the instrument costs.

LADY-IN-WAITING 2:   You'd better put boots on before you go through all that mud.

LADY-IN-WAITING 1:   Hello there, Swineherd. How much is the pot?

PRINCE/SWINEHERD: I must have ten kisses from the princess.

LADY-IN-WAITING 1:   (shocked) Heaven prepare us!

PRINCE/SWINEHERD: I won't take less.

PRINCESS: Well, what did he say?

LADY-IN-WAITING 1:   I really cannot tell you! It is so shocking!

PRINCESS: Then you must whisper it.

LADY-IN-WAITING 1:   (whisper to princess)

PRINCESS: What a wretch! Let's be off.

NARRATOR 2:   But she hadn't gone very far when she heard the pot's song.

NARRATORS 1 AND 2:   (motion to audience to begin singing)

AUDIENCE: Ach du lieber Augustin
Alles ist weg, weg, weg!

PRINCESS: Go and ask him if he'll take ten kisses from my ladies-in-waiting.

LADY-IN-WAITING 3:   Will you take ten kisses from us?

PRINCE/SWINEHERD: No thank you. Ten kisses from the princess, or I keep the pot.

PRINCESS: How tiresome. Then you will have to stand around me so that no one sees.

NARRATOR 1:   So the ladies-in-waiting stood around her and spread out their skirts while the swineherd took his ten kisses.

LADIES-IN-WAITING 1, 2, AND 3:   (stand in front of the princess and prince/swineherd and count to ten slowly)

NARRATOR 2:   Now the princess and the ladies had the pot. What a delight. The pot was kept boiling day and night. They knew what was cooking on every stove in the town from the chamberlains to the shoemakers. The ladies-in-waiting danced about and clapped their hands.

LADY-IN-WAITING 1:   (joyfully) We know who has the sweet soup and pancakes for dinner, and who has cutlets. How amusing.

LADY-IN-WAITING 2:   (haughtily) Highly interesting.

LADY-IN-WAITING 3:   What a joy.

PRINCESS: Quiet. Remember, I am the emperor's daughter.

Scene Three

NARRATOR 2:   Now the swineherd, who was really the prince, did not remain idle. Now he made a rattle. When it was swung around it played all the waltzes, gallops, and jig tunes which have been heard since the beginning of the world.

NARRATOR 1:   The princess walked by the pigsty with her ladies and heard the rattle.

PRINCESS: How superbe! I have never heard finer music. Go and ask him how much it costs, but no more kisses.

NARRATOR 1:   The lady-in-waiting reported to the princess,

LADY-IN-WAITING 1:   He wants 100 kisses from the princess!

PRINCESS: Why, he must be mad.

NARRATOR 2:   She started to walk away but then she stopped.

PRINCESS: One really must encourage art. Go and ask him if he'll take ten kisses the same as yesterday and he can take the rest from the ladies-in-waiting.

LADY-IN-WAITING 1:   (horrified) Oh no. I won't like that.

LADY-IN-WAITING 2:   (horrified) I don't want to.

43

LADY-IN-WAITING 3: (horrified) I can't do that.

PRINCESS: (impatiently) Oh nonsense! I'm the emperor's daughter. If I can kiss him you can do the same.

NARRATOR 1: So the lady-in-waiting asked the swineherd.

PRINCE/SWINEHERD: A hundred kisses from the princess, or each keeps his own.

PRINCESS: Stand in front of me.

LADIES-IN-WAITING 1, 2, AND 3: (stand in front of the princess and swineherd)

NARRATOR 2: Now the emperor was standing on the balcony and he chanced to look out at the pigsty.

EMPEROR: Whatever is going on over at the pigsty? Why, it's the ladies-in-waiting. What game are they playing? I must go and see.

NARRATOR 1: So the emperor pulled on his slippers which were down-trodden at the heels and hurried as fast as he could to the pigsty.

NARRATOR 2: When he got to the yard he walked ever so softly. The ladies were very busy counting the kisses so there would not be too many or too few. They never heard the emperor.

EMPEROR: What is all this?

NARRATOR 2: The ladies-in-waiting were just counting the 86th kiss.

LADIES-IN-WAITING 1, 2, AND 3: (shout together) 86!

NARRATOR 2: The emperor took off one of his slippers and spanked the princess.

EMPEROR: Out you go!

NARRATOR 1: And there were the princess and the swineherd outside the emperor's kingdom and the gate locked.

NARRATOR 2: The princess cried and the swineherd scolded and the rain poured down.

PRINCESS: Oh miserable creature that I am! If only I had accepted the handsome prince. How unhappy I am.

NARRATOR 1: The swineherd went behind a tree. He wiped the stain from his face and threw away his ugly clothes. Then he stepped out from behind the tree dressed as a prince.

PRINCESS: (surprised) Oh, it is you, the prince! (curtsies)

PRINCE: (in a superior voice) I have come to despise thee. Thou wouldst not have an honorable prince, thou could not prize a rose or a nightingale, but thou wouldst kiss a swineherd for a pot and a music box.

NARRATOR 2: The prince went back to his own little kingdom and shut and locked the door.

NARRATOR 1:   The princess had to stand outside and sing,

NARRATORS 1 AND 2:   (motion to audience to sing)

AUDIENCE: Ach du lieber Augustin,
        Alles ist weg, weg, weg!

Sometimes Arthur Is Choosy

BY BERNARD WABER

SOMETIMES ARTHUR IS CHOOSY

It might be difficult for you to imitate an anteater because you probably don't know many anteaters personally. Don't worry, there are many similarities between Arthur and a little boy or girl. You might even recognize his mother. She might remind you of your own mom. More stories about Arthur can be found in *An Anteater Named Arthur.*

Players: 3

Narrator   Mother   Arthur

NARRATOR: I am _____ .
        I read the narrator.

MOTHER: I am _____ .
        I play Arthur's mother.

ARTHUR: I am _____ .
        I play Arthur.

NARRATOR: We are going to present a play called "Sometimes Arthur Is Choosy." It is from the book *An Anteater Named Arthur* by Bernard Waber.

MOTHER: (calls) Breakfast! Breakfast is ready, Arthur.

NARRATOR: Arthur comes downstairs.

48

ARTHUR: What are we having, Mother?

MOTHER: We are having ants.

ARTHUR: What kind of ants?

MOTHER: The red ones.

NARRATOR: Arthur makes a face.

ARTHUR: (makes a face)

MOTHER: But look at them. Aren't these the most beautiful ants you have ever seen in all your life? I gathered them especially for you.

NARRATOR: Arthur looks and makes another face.

ARTHUR: (makes another face)

MOTHER: Arthur, red ants are delicious and so good for you. Don't you want to grow up to be big and strong, as big and strong as your father? Have you watched your father eat red ants?

NARRATOR: Arthur makes more faces.

ARTHUR: (makes more faces)

MOTHER: I have an idea. Shall I sprinkle sugar on them? Red ants are simply delightful with sugar.

NARRATOR: Arthur shakes his head.

ARTHUR: (shakes head)

MOTHER: A twist of lemon, perhaps?

NARRATOR: Arthur shakes his head again.

ARTHUR: (shakes his head)

MOTHER: Arthur, red ants aren't exactly easy to come by! You have to scratch mighty deep for red ants.

NARRATOR: Arthur begins playing with his spoon.

ARTHUR: (plays with imaginary spoon)

MOTHER: You ought to at least try one. You will never know if you like something unless you give it a chance. Here, how about this one?

ARTHUR: ILK!

MOTHER: · Very well! Never mind about the red ants. Never mind that you are missing out on the world's tastiest, most delicious, most scrumptious dish. What will you have for breakfast instead?

ARTHUR: (happily) Brown ants!

NARRATOR: The End.

Animal Antics

Here is a set of poems and jokes that makes a fun presentation piece. Ask each reader to introduce his or her poem by announcing the title and author before beginning.

Monkeys
Readers: 2

MONKEY

by Sylvia Read

READER 1:   If you and I could ever meet
A monkey going down the street,
And I were you and you were he—
Why, then the monkey would be me!

THE MONKEY AND YOU

by Julie Holder

READER 2:   I am a monkey
In a zoo.
You stare at me
I stare at you.
Two sides to these bars there are.
What is life like over there
In your zoo?
At least you have peanuts to spare,
Who throws the peanuts to you?

51

Ants

Readers: 2

ADVICE
Anonymous

READER 1:   Don't sit on an ant-hill,
Whatever you do;
The ants won't like it
And neither will you.

ANT

by X. J. Kennedy

READER 2:   An ant works hard
Hauling great weight
In our back yard,

But you can't
Hear an ant
Pant.

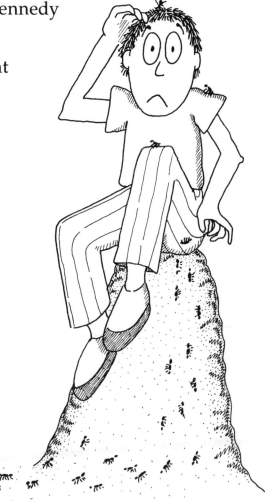

Tigers

Readers: 2

TIGER

by John Gardner

READER 1: The Tiger is a perfect saint
As long as you respect him;
But if he happens to say *ain't*,
You'd better not correct him.

TIGER

by Mary Ann Hoberman

READER 2: I'm a tiger
Striped with fur
Don't come near
Or I might GRRR
Don't come near
Or I might growl
Don't come near
Or I might
BITE!

Porcupines

Readers: 2

WHO TO PET AND WHO NOT TO
by X. J. Kennedy

READER 1: Go pet a kitten, pet a dog,
Go pet a worm for practice,
But don't go pet a porcupine—
You want to be a cactus?

THE PORCUPINE
by Karla Kuskin

READER 2: A porcupine looks somewhat silly,
He also is extremely quilly
And if he shoots a quill at you
Run fast
Or you'll be quilly too.

I would not want a porcupine
To be my loving valentine.

Bugs

Readers: 5

COCKROACH
by Yoshiko Uchida

READER 1: "Cockroach"

READER 2: by Yoshiko Uchida

READER 1: Hurrying

READER 2: Scurrying

READER 3: Escaping
Cockroach,

READER 1: WHAM!

READER 2: SLAM!

READER 3: I squash you
Into nothingness,
Pleased.

READER 1: But then, I wonder,

READER 2: Was a tiny
Baby roach
Waiting for you

READER 3: Somewhere
In the damp
Darkness
Beneath
My sink?

A BUG

by Karla Kuskin

READER 4: "A Bug" by Karla Kuskin

READER 5: A bug sat in a silver flower
Thinking silver thoughts

READER 4: A bigger bug out for a walk
Climbed up that silver flower stalk
And snapped the small bug down his jaws

READER 5: Without a pause
Without a care
For all the bug's small silver thoughts.

READER 4: It isn't right

READER 5: It isn't fair

READER 4: That bug ate that little bug
Because that little bug was there.

READER 5: He also ate his underwear.

Animal Jokes

Readers: 3 per joke

NARRATOR: An explorer asked his guide a question:

EXPLORER: I'd enjoy a swim in this lagoon. Are you sure no alligators live in there?

GUIDE: Oh yes. I'm sure. All the sharks have scared them away.

NARRATOR: A mother and son were talking:

MOTHER: Did you give the goldfish fresh water?

SON: No. They didn't drink all the water I gave them yesterday.

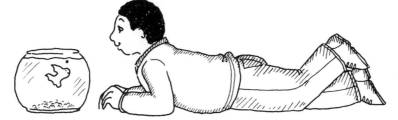

NARRATOR: A student asked a teacher a question.

STUDENT: Is it true that tigers won't attack you if you carry a flashlight?

TEACHER: It depends on how fast you run with the flashlight.

NARRATOR: A theatrical agent received a call from an anxious actor.

ACTOR: Can you use me? I know all the plays of Shakespeare by heart.

THEATRICAL AGENT: I know ten actors who can do that.

ACTOR: I can play all the works of Mozart on a comb while standing on my head.

THEATRICAL AGENT: I know 20 actors who can do that.

ACTOR: I can dance on the ceiling while playing a harp.

THEATRICAL AGENT: Sorry, I'm not interested.

ACTOR: Don't hang up. There's one thing I still haven't told you. I'm a dog.

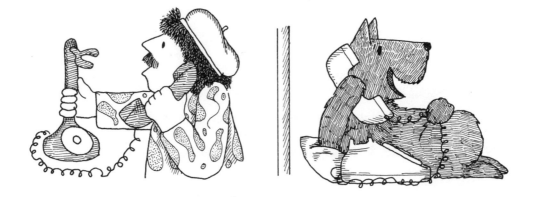

NARRATOR: A mother lion was talking to a baby lion.

MOTHER LION: What are you doing?

LITTLE LION: Chasing a hunter around the forest.

MOTHER LION: I've told you a million times, don't play with your food.

NARRATOR: Two dogs were talking.

FIRST DOG: My name is Rex. What's yours?

SECOND DOG: I don't know, but I think it's Bad Dog.

NARRATOR: Two friends were talking.

HILARY: Did I ever tell you about the time I met a lion?

BROOKE: No. What happened?

HILARY: Well. There I was. I had no gun and the lion was growling ferociously and clawing the ground.

BROOKE: What did you do?

HILARY: I just moved on to the elephant cage.

NARRATOR: Two sheep were having a conversation:

SHEEP 1:   Baa, baa.

SHEEP 2:   Moo moo.

SHEEP 1:   What do you mean, moo moo? You're a sheep.

SHEEP 2:   Yes, but I'm learning a foreign language.

Somersaults and Headstands

By Kathleen Fraser

Readers: 2

READERS 1 AND 2: "Somersaults and Headstands" by Kathleen Fraser

READER 1: What are you doing?

READER 2: I'm turning a somersault.

READER 1: How do you do it?

READER 2: I put my head in the grass and roll over like a snail.

READER 1: Could you turn a wintersault?

READER 2: No, because my head would get cold in the snow.

READER 1: Now, what are you doing?

READER 2: A headstand.

READER 1: Is it like a somersault?

READER 2: Well, sort of, but you stop in the middle.

READER 1: How do you keep from falling?

READER 2: I pretend everyone else is walking upside down.

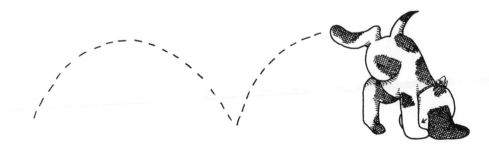

The Skipping Pot

THE SKIPPING POT

"The Skipping Pot" is a Danish story, but the same tale exists in the folklore of many cultures. The basic plot is that one belonging, here a cow, is exchanged for a seemingly worthless object, which then turns out to be of great value. Everyone is familiar with the most famous version of this tale, "Jack and the Beanstalk." With this story, the more ordinary the object traded for, the more magical the final outcome of the tale.

Players: 10

Narrator 1	Farmer	Cow	Pot	Field Hand
Narrator 2	Wife	Stranger	Cook	Rich Man

NARRATOR 1: I am _____.
   I am a narrator.

NARRATOR 2: I am _____.
   I am also a narrator.

FARMER: I am _____.
   I play the farmer.

WIFE: I am _____.
   I play the farmer's wife.

COW: I am _____.
   I play the cow.

STRANGER: I am _____.
   I play the stranger.

POT: I am _____.
   I play the pot.

COOK: I am _____.
   I play the cook.

FIELD HAND: I am _____.
   I play the field hand.

RICH MAN: I am _____.
   I play the rich man.

NARRATOR 2: Welcome to our presentation of "The Skipping Pot."

NARRATOR 1: There was once a poor farmer . . .

NARRATOR 2: who had a wife.

NARRATOR 1: They had a cow . . .

COW: Moo.

WIFE: Husband, we must sell the cow. We need money for food.

FARMER: You are right, Wife. Come along, Cow.

COW: Moo.

STRANGER: Good morning, sir. What a fine cow you have there.

FARMER: He is for sale for only ten gulden.

STRANGER: I have no money to give you but I have this pot.

FARMER: No thank you. We need money.

POT: Please take me. You'll not be sorry.

FARMER: A talking pot. If you can talk, you must be able to do other things too.

NARRATOR 1: The farmer exchanged the pot for the cow and said goodbye to his cow.

FARMER: Bye, Cow.

COW: Moo.

NARRATOR 1: The farmer brought the pot home to his wife.

FARMER: Look, Wife. I have traded our cow for this pot.

WIFE: Silly man. What good is a pot?

POT: I'm very useful. You shall see.

WIFE: A talking pot?

POT: I skip! I skip!

WIFE: Where do you skip?

POT: I skip to the rich man's house.

NARRATOR 2: The pot skipped out of the door and up the path to the rich man's house. The cook was preparing a plum pudding.

COOK: What have we here? The perfect pot for my pudding.

NARRATOR 2: The cook put the pudding into the pot.

POT: I skip! I skip!

COOK: Where do you skip?

POT: Home. Home to my friends.

NARRATOR 2: The cook just had time to say . . .

COOK: Wait!

NARRATOR 2: before the pot skipped back to the farmer's house. The farmer and his wife were overjoyed to see the pot.

WIFE: Welcome, Pot. What a fine pudding you have brought.

FARMER: What a fine meal we will have.

NARRATOR 2: The farmer and his wife ate the pudding and cleaned the pot.

POT: I skip! I skip!

WIFE: Where do you skip?

POT: To the rich man's house.

NARRATOR 1: The pot skipped to the rich man's barn. The field hand was getting ready to store a wagonload of grain.

FIELD HAND: What have we here? The perfect pot for this grain.

NARRATOR 1: The field hand put some of the grain into the pot.

POT: I skip! I skip!

FIELD HAND: Where do you skip?

POT: Home. Home to my friends.

NARRATOR 1:   The field hand just had time to say . . .

FIELD HAND: Wait!

NARRATOR 1:   before the pot skipped back to the farmer's house.

FARMER: Welcome, Pot. What a fine load of grain you have brought.

WIFE: Enough grain to make bread for a long time.

NARRATOR 1:   The farmer and his wife stored the grain and cleaned the pot.

POT: I skip! I skip!

WIFE: Where do you skip?

POT: To the rich man's house.

NARRATOR 2:   The pot skipped to the rich man's house and right into the treasure room.

RICH MAN: What have we here? The perfect pot for my money.

NARRATOR 2:   The rich man filled the pot with gold coins.

POT: I skip! I skip!

RICH MAN: Where do you skip?

POT: Home. Home to my friends.

NARRATOR 2:   The rich man just had time to say . . .

RICH MAN: Wait!

NARRATOR 2:   before the pot skipped back to the farmer's house.

WIFE: Welcome, Pot. What a big load of gold you have brought.

FARMER: That is a lot of gold. Thank you, Pot.

NARRATOR 2:   The farmer and his wife lived happily for many years, and the pot stayed in a corner and slept.

POT: My skipping days are over.

NARRATOR 1:   The End.

ADMIT ONE

THE SKIPPING POT

If We Walked on Our Hands

by Beatrice Schenk de Regniers

Readers: 6

READER 6: "If We Walked on Our Hands" by Beatrice Schenk de Regniers

READER 1: If we walked on our hands instead of our feet

READER 2: And we all ate paper instead of meat

ALL: What a mixed-up place this world would be
What a mixed-up
   fixed-up
   topsy-turvy
   sit-u-a-tion.

READER 3: If we wore our hats on our behinds

READER 4: And all we ate were melon rinds

ALL: What a mixed-up place this world would be
What a mixed-up
   fixed-up
   topsy-turvy
   sit-u-a-tion.

READER 5: If babies worked while papas played

READER 6: If the children gave orders
and parents obeyed

ALL: What a mixed-up place this world would be
What a mixed-up
   fixed-up
   topsy-turvy
   sit-u-a-tion.

The Bridge
over the River Clarinette

BY PIERRE GAMARRA

translated by Paulette Henderson

THE BRIDGE OVER THE RIVER CLARINETTE

There are several versions of this legend in which the devil helps build a bridge for a French town. In most of the tales, the devil is foiled in his attempt to outwit the townspeople. In "The Bridge over the River Clarinette," the townspeople learn—too late—an important lesson.

Players: 7

Narrator 1	Monsieur Leopold	Mayor
Narrator 2	Madame Barbette	Teacher
	Stranger	

NARRATOR 1: Greetings. We would like to tell you the story of "The Bridge over the River Clarinette." I am _____ and I am one of your narrators.

NARRATOR 2: I am _____ and I also am a narrator.

M. LEOPOLD: I am _____ and I play the innkeeper, Monsieur Leopold.

MME. BARBETTE: I am _____ and I play the grocer, Madame Barbette.

MAYOR: I am _____ and I play the mayor.

70

TEACHER: I am _____
and I play the teacher.

STRANGER: I am _____
and I play the stranger.

NARRATOR 1: The inhabitants of the little town of Framboisy-sur-Clarinette were worried. The bridge that spanned the River Clarinette was about to collapse.

NARRATOR 2: And if the bridge should collapse, the citizens of Framboisy would have no more trade, no more traffic, no more tourists.

NARRATOR 1: It was therefore necessary to reconstruct the bridge.

NARRATOR 2: But Framboisy was poor, and so the town council was deeply troubled. This morning Monsieur Leopold, owner of the Green Swan Inn, greeted Madame Barbette, the grocer.

M. LEOPOLD: Bonjour. How are things with you this morning, Madame Barbette?

MME. BARBETTE: Very bad, Monsieur Leopold. Business is falling off. I did not sell more than one package of macaroni last week. People just don't have any money anymore.

M. LEOPOLD: (sighing) As for me, I don't have any customers either. The tourists don't dare cross the bridge nowadays.

71

MME. BARBETTE: Did it split last night?

M. LEOPOLD: Yes it did; I heard it. It's a disgrace. It could cave in at any moment.

MME. BARBETTE: What's to become of us? What we need is a new bridge.

NARRATOR 1: At that moment Monsieur Leopold and Madame Barbette saw the mayor and the teacher coming out of the town hall.

M. LEOPOLD: Well, well, how are town matters going? Are we going to rebuild the bridge?

NARRATOR 2: The mayor shook his head with infinite sadness.

MAYOR: The council has examined various bridge plans. But it's an outrageously expensive undertaking. We'll never be able to pay for it.

MME. BARBETTE: Nevertheless, you must make a decision. Without a bridge we're ruined. No one dares to venture across our dilapidated old bridge.

NARRATOR 1: The teacher shaded his eyes and gazed in the direction of the bridge.

TEACHER: Someone is coming.

M. LEOPOLD: A stranger! Impossible! He wasn't afraid to cross.

TEACHER: Amazing. But what an odd sort of person, all dressed in red and black and hopping from side to side. Look at his strange, uncanny smile and the glint in his eyes.

NARRATOR 2: The stranger approached the group and bowed to each of the citizens with great respect. His eyes glowed like deep red rubies.

STRANGER: I am very honored to be visiting the distinguished inhabitants of Framboisy-sur-Clarinette.

M. LEOPOLD: Monsieur is traveling?

STRANGER: I'm going about the country on business.

TEACHER: Are you a businessman?

STRANGER: Yes. I buy and I sell.

MME. BARBETTE: And what is it that you sell?

STRANGER: Anything and everything.

MME. BARBETTE: Anything and everything?

STRANGER: Yes, anything at all. Sausages, cars, houses, shirts, bridges . . .

MAYOR: Did you say bridges? You sell bridges?

STRANGER: But of course. Bridges. All sorts of bridges. Big ones, small ones, medium-sized ones. Made of wood, iron, even concrete.

MAYOR: It just so happens that we are in need of a bridge. A solid bridge with two or three arches.

STRANGER: (laughing) Easy.

MME. BARBETTE: (defiantly) And what is the price of a bridge?

STRANGER: Nothing at all.

NARRATOR 1: The four citizens of Framboisy jumped for joy, but the teacher said,

TEACHER: That can't be true. If you build us a new bridge certainly you will ask for something in exchange.

STRANGER: Almost nothing.

TEACHER: What would you ask of us?

STRANGER: Your words. You give me your words, and I will build you a beautiful bridge in five seconds. Note that I am not asking for *all* of your words; I will leave you a few for your daily needs—drink, eat, sleep, bread, butter, coffee . . .

TEACHER: But what will you do with our words?

STRANGER: That's *my* business. Promise that you will give me your words, and I will build you a bridge—a magnificent concrete and steel bridge guaranteed for ten centuries.

TEACHER: If you take our words we will find it very difficult to converse.

STRANGER: No, no, no. I will leave you enough to satisfy you. I'll leave you the most important words. And you shall

74

have an extraordinary bridge in five seconds.

M. LEOPOLD: Are you a magician?

STRANGER: (modestly) I have a very advanced technique at my disposal.

M. LEOPOLD: We could try it.

MME. BARBETTE: All right. Let him have our words, and we shall have the bridge.

TEACHER: I object. We should never give up our words. We won't be able to hold a conversation.

M. LEOPOLD: Let us try it.

STRANGER: You agree? I leave you a few words—bread, butter, milk, coffee, eat, drink, sleep, house, chair—and I will build you an extraordinary bridge.

MME. BARBETTE, MAYOR, AND M. LEOPOLD: (together) Agreed.

NARRATOR 2:   The teacher shook his head, but it was too late.

NARRATOR 1:   The stranger pointed his finger at the old bridge and instantaneously a new, beautiful, three-arched bridge rose into the sky.

NARRATOR 2:   The mayor nudged the innkeeper and said,

MAYOR: Bread. Butter. Eat. Drink.

NARRATOR 1:   The innkeeper looked at him and replied,

M. LEOPOLD: Drink. Sleep. House. Chair.

MAYOR: Butter. Bread. Eat.

MME..BARBETTE: Sleep. Coffee. Butter.

TEACHER: The End?

Ali Baba
and Princess Farrah

from Ali Baba Bernstein

BY JOHANNA HURWITZ

ALI BABA AND PRINCESS FARRAH

The old fairy tales have been told and retold many times over the years. Now these tales are so well known to both children and adults that many contemporary authors enjoy using them in their stories. In this chapter from *Ali Baba Bernstein*, the story of the frog who turned into a prince when he was kissed by a gentle princess is given a humorous, contemporary twist.

Johanna Hurwitz has written wonderful books for children. If you haven't read her funny stories about Aldo and Nora and Teddy, you probably should—you'll love them!

Players: 5

| Narrator 1 | Valerie | Farrah, a frog |
| Narrator 2 | Ali Baba | (real or imagined) |

NARRATOR 1: I'm _____
    and I play a narrator.

NARRATOR 2: I'm _____
    and I also play a narrator.

VALERIE: I'm _____
    and I play Valerie.

ALI BABA: I'm _____
    and I play Ali Baba.

FARRAH: I'm _____
    and I play the frog (ribbit!).

NARRATOR 1:   David Bernstein was eight years, five months, and seventeen days old when he chose his new name. You see, there were already four Davids in his third-grade class. There were *seventeen* David Bernsteins in the Manhattan telephone book! So, he decided he would choose a new name from one of his favorite books, *The Arabian Nights*. He chose Ali Baba, and that is how he became known as Ali Baba Bernstein.

NARRATOR 2:   One Sunday, Ali Baba and his parents went to visit their friends, the Fishbones. At least, Ali Baba's parents were friends with the Fishbones. Ali Baba wasn't at all sure he would like Valerie, the Fishbones' daughter.

NARRATOR 1:   Valerie and Ali Baba are in Valerie's bedroom.

VALERIE: I have a frog. Her name is Farrah.

ALI BABA: Did you ever think that maybe Farrah isn't a frog at all?

VALERIE: Of course Farrah is a frog. Anyone with two eyes can see that.

ALI BABA: Oh, something can look like a frog if it has been enchanted into becoming a frog. But Farrah could be a prince.

VALERIE: A prince?

ALI BABA: Didn't you ever hear the story of the Frog Prince? It's about a handsome prince who was turned into a frog by a wicked witch.

VALERIE: Of course I know that story, but Farrah is just a plain, ordinary frog. She's not a prince.

ALI BABA: Did you ever try?

VALERIE: Try what?

ALI BABA: Kissing the frog.

VALERIE: (making a face) I couldn't kiss her. I might get germs or something.

ALI BABA: Then you'll never know. Farrah might really be a handsome prince. He might even have looked like Christopher Reeve or John Travolta before the enchantment. And you never cared enough to find out. He might even die, and it will be all your fault.

VALERIE: (uncertainly) I found this frog on a trip to Bear Mountain. Suppose I hadn't found it. Then what?

ALI BABA: Then some other girl would have found him. And she probably would have kissed him. Instead, he's had to sit in the dirt and eat bugs. If you love him, kiss him.

NARRATOR 1:   Slowly, Valerie brought the frog closer to her.

FARRAH: (hops close to Valerie)

VALERIE: (frowning) It can't be a prince. There isn't any more magic nowadays.

ALI BABA: Kiss the frog, Valerie.

NARRATOR 2:   Valerie took a deep breath and puckered her lips. She kissed the frog on the forehead.

VALERIE: (kisses frog on the forehead)

ALI BABA: (laughing) I made you kiss a frog! You should have seen your face. And you thought it would turn into a prince.

VALERIE: No, I didn't. I knew it wouldn't. It's a girl frog. It needs to be kissed by a boy. Then it will turn into a princess.

ALI BABA: (backing away) Fat chance.

VALERIE: There's only one way to find out.

NARRATOR 1:   Valerie gently pushed the frog towards Ali Baba.

FARRAH: (hops closer to Ali Baba)

VALERIE: This is a female frog. I took her to a pet shop and they told me. She's been waiting for a boy to kiss her and end the enchantment. My father couldn't do it because he's already married. You must break the spell for her.

ALI BABA: Come off it, Valerie. Let's put the frog away and play a game.

VALERIE: You want to play a game while this poor princess is sitting in the dirt? You really are a mean person, Ali Baba. Luckily for Farrah, my cousin Lloyd is coming to visit next week. He's older than you are and better looking, too. Farrah would prefer to be a princess for him and not for you, anyhow.

ALI BABA: How old is Lloyd?

VALERIE: Ten. Practically eleven, actually.

NARRATOR 2:   Ali Baba thought for a moment. It couldn't hurt to kiss a frog. It might be an interesting experience. Why not? Gently his lips brushed Farrah's skin.

ALI BABA: (leans down and kisses Farrah)

NARRATOR 1: Nothing happened. Ali Baba rubbed his lips on his sleeve. At least Valerie didn't laugh, he thought.

VALERIE: Hey, you're a good sport! My mother bought éclairs because you and your parents were coming. Do you want some?

ALI BABA: Sure.

NARRATOR 2: Ali Baba wanted to get away from all this kissing.

NARRATOR 1: Ali Baba put Farrah back in her tank,

ALI BABA: (puts Farrah in her tank)

NARRATOR 1: and Ali Baba and Valerie went into the kitchen and each had a big, chocolate, custard-filled pastry and a glass of milk. It wasn't going to be such a bad day after all!

NARRATOR 2: The End.

ADMIT ONE

ALI BABA AND PRINCESS FARRAH

Food: A Triplet

TOY TIK KA
by Charlotte Pomerantz

Readers: 2

READER 1: "Toy Tik Ka"

READER 2: by Charlotte Pomerantz

READER 1: I like fish.

READER 2: Toy tik ka.

READER 1: I like chicken.

READER 2: Toy tik ga.

READER 1: I like duck.

READER 2: Toy tik veet.

READER 1: I like meat.

READER 2: Toy tik teet.

READER 1: But though I like

READER 2: Ka, ga, veet, teet

BOTH: Fish and chicken, duck and meat
Best of all I like to eat.

PECULIAR
by Eve Merriam

Readers: 2

READER 1: "Peculiar"

READER 2: by Eve Merriam

READER 1: I once knew a boy who was odd as could be:

READER 2: He liked to eat cauliflower and broccoli
And spinach and turnips and rhubarb pies

READER 1: And he didn't like hamburgers or French fries.

JUMP ROPE RHYME
by Charlie Meehan
Readers: 7

ALL: "Jump Rope Rhyme" by Charlie Meehan

READER 1: Chocolate ice cream,

READER 2: Chocolate cake,

READER 3: Chocolate cookies,

READER 4: Chocolate shake,

READER 5: Chocolate bagels,

READER 6: Chocolate steak,

READER 7: Make a chocolate belly ache!

READER 1: Faster!

ALL: Chocolate ice cream,
Chocolate cake,
Chocolate cookies,
Chocolate shake,
Chocolate bagels,
Chocolate steak,
Make a chocolate belly ache!

Bringing News
from Home

This is a delightful play for two people. The story is such a ridiculous one that you will enjoy watching your audience smile as people begin to catch on to the joke and finally laugh aloud as the punch line is delivered.

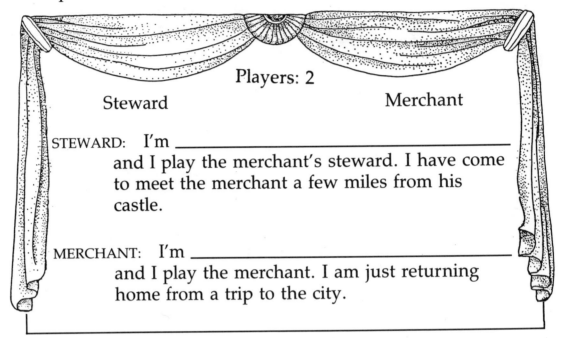

Players: 2

Steward   Merchant

STEWARD: I'm _____
and I play the merchant's steward. I have come to meet the merchant a few miles from his castle.

MERCHANT: I'm _____
and I play the merchant. I am just returning home from a trip to the city.

STEWARD: Greetings, sir. Welcome home.

MERCHANT: Hello, Steward. What's the news from home?

STEWARD: Oh, sir, your dog has died.

MERCHANT: I'm so sorry to hear that. How did she die?

STEWARD: I expect it was from eating too much horse meat.

MERCHANT: Whatever do you mean? Where did she find so much horse meat?

STEWARD: Well, sir, all your horses are dead.

MERCHANT: Dead. I don't understand. How so?

STEWARD: They died from overwork, after hauling all that water.

MERCHANT: Water? What water?

STEWARD: The water we used for putting out the fire.

MERCHANT: The fire? What fire is that?

STEWARD: The fire that burned down your castle.

MERCHANT: My castle is gone? What do you mean? How did the fire start?

STEWARD: It was probably the torches.

MERCHANT: The torches? When were torches used?

STEWARD: To light the way for your mother's funeral.

MERCHANT: What do you mean? My mother is dead?

STEWARD: Yes, sir. I'm so sorry. She died of a broken heart when she heard about your father's death.

MERCHANT: My father is dead too? How did he die?

STEWARD: It was the shock, sir, when he heard about it.

MERCHANT: Heard about what?

STEWARD: The bank failing.

87

MERCHANT: Our bank has failed? I have no more money?

STEWARD: Yes, sir. The dog is dead. The horses are dead. The castle has burned down. Your mother is dead. Your father is dead, and your money is gone. So, I just thought I'd come meet you and bring you the news from home.

MERCHANT AND STEWARD: The End.

Beyond Expectations

from *The Phantom Tollbooth*

BY NORTON JUSTER

Norton Juster's *The Phantom Tollbooth* is considered a modern classic. Although it appears to be silly and nonsensical, it actually has a lot to say about math, language, and, in this chapter, thinking.

This is a long, somewhat sophisticated play, one probably most appropriate for an older group. If you have a little time for rehearsal, the lethargarians should practice together so that they become a closely knit chorus of sleepy players.

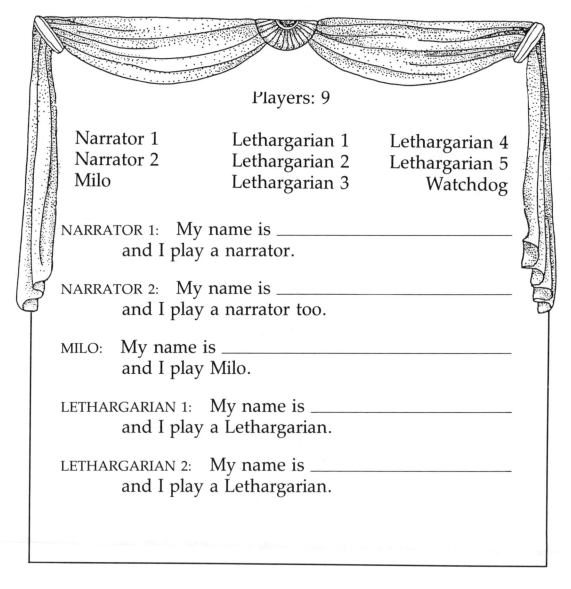

Players: 9

Narrator 1	Lethargarian 1	Lethargarian 4
Narrator 2	Lethargarian 2	Lethargarian 5
Milo	Lethargarian 3	Watchdog

NARRATOR 1:   My name is _____
and I play a narrator.

NARRATOR 2:   My name is _____
and I play a narrator too.

MILO: My name is _____
and I play Milo.

LETHARGARIAN 1:   My name is _____
and I play a Lethargarian.

LETHARGARIAN 2:   My name is _____
and I play a Lethargarian.

LETHARGARIAN 3:   My name is _____
        and I play a Lethargarian.

LETHARGARIAN 4:   My name is _____
        and I play a Lethargarian.

LETHARGARIAN 5:   My name is _____
        and I also play a Lethargarian.

WATCHDOG: My name is _____
        and I play the watchdog.

NARRATOR 1:   Milo's car stopped and wouldn't budge another
        inch.

MILO: (worried) I wonder where I am?

LETHARGARIAN 1:   (from offstage) You're . . . in . . . the . . . Dol
        . . . drums.

NARRATOR 1:   Milo looked around quickly to see who had spo-
        ken. No one was there, and it was as quiet and still as one
        could imagine.

LETHARGARIAN 2:   (yawning) Yes . . . the . . . Doldrums.

MILO: (loudly) What are the Doldrums?

LETHARGARIAN 3:   The Doldrums, my young friend, are where
        nothing ever happens and nothing ever changes.

NARRATOR 2:   The voice came from so close that Milo jumped with surprise, for, sitting on his right shoulder, so lightly that he hardly noticed, was a small creature exactly the color of his shirt.

LETHARGARIAN 3:   Allow me to introduce all of us. We are the Lethargarians at your service.

NARRATOR 2:   Milo looked around and, for the first time, noticed dozens of them—sitting on the car, standing in the road, and lying all over the trees and bushes. They were very difficult to see, because whatever they happened to be sitting on or near was exactly the color they happened to be.

NARRATOR 1:   Each one looked very much like the other (except for the color, of course), and some looked even more like each other than they did like themselves.

MILO: I'm very pleased to meet you. I think I'm lost. Can you help me please?

LETHARGARIAN 1:   Don't say "think." It's against the law.

NARRATOR 2:   The Lethargarian on his shoulder had fallen asleep. This one yawned and fell off to sleep, too.

LETHARGARIAN 4:   (dozing off) No one's allowed to think in the Doldrums.

NARRATOR 1:   As each one spoke, he fell asleep and another picked up the conversation with hardly any interruption.

LETHARGARIAN 5: Don't you have a rule book? It's local ordinance 175389-J.

NARRATOR 2: Milo quickly pulled the rule book from his pocket, opened to the page, and read,

MILO: Ordinance 175389-J: It shall be unlawful, illegal, and unethical to think, think of thinking, surmise, presume, reason, meditate, or speculate while in the Doldrums. Anyone breaking this law shall be severely punished!

(indignantly) That's a ridiculous law. Everybody thinks.

LETHARGARIAN 2: (shouting) We don't!

LETHARGARIAN 1: And most of the time *you* don't, that's why you're here. You weren't thinking, and you weren't paying attention either. People who don't pay attention often get stuck in the Doldrums.

NARRATOR 1: And with that he fell snoring into the grass.

NARRATOR 2: Milo couldn't help laughing at the little creatures' strange behavior, even though he knew it might be rude.

LETHARGARIAN 4: Stop that at once. Laughing is against the law. Don't you have a rule book? It's local ordinance 574381-W.

NARRATOR 2: Milo found Ordinance 574381-W.

MILO: In the Doldrums, laughter is frowned upon and smiling is permitted only on alternate Thursdays. Violators shall be dealt with most harshly.

Well, if you can't laugh or think, what can you do?

LETHARGARIAN 5: Anything as long as it's nothing, and everything as long as it isn't anything. There's lots to do; we have a very busy schedule.

LETHARGARIAN 1: At 8 o'clock we get up, and then we spend

LETHARGARIAN 2: from 8 to 9 daydreaming.

LETHARGARIAN 3: From 9 to 9:30 we take our early midmorning nap.

LETHARGARIAN 4: From 9:30 to 10:30 we dawdle and delay.

LETHARGARIAN 5: From 10:30 to 11:30 we take our late early morning nap.

LETHARGARIAN 1: From 11:30 to 12:00 we bide our time and then eat lunch.

LETHARGARIAN 2: From 1:00 to 2:00 we linger and loiter.

LETHARGARIAN 3: From 2:00 to 2:30 we take our early afternoon nap.

LETHARGARIAN 4: From 2:30 to 3:30 we put off for tomorrow what we could have done today.

LETHARGARIAN 5: From 3:30 to 4:00 we take our early late afternoon nap.

LETHARGARIAN 1:   From 4:00 to 5:00 we loaf and lounge until dinner.

LETHARGARIAN 2:   From 6:00 to 7:00 we dilly dally.

LETHARGARIAN 4:   As you can see, that leaves almost no time for brooding, lagging, plodding, or procrastinating, and if we stopped to think or laugh, we'd never get nothing done.

MILO: You mean you'd never get anything done.

LETHARGARIAN 1:   We don't want to get anything done. We want to get nothing done, and we can do that without your help.

LETHARGARIAN 2:   You see, it's really quite strenuous doing nothing all day, so once a week we take a holiday and go nowhere, which was just where we were going when you came along. Would you care to join us?

LETHARGARIAN 3:   From 7:00 to 8:00 we take our early evening nap, and then for an hour before we go to bed at 9:00 we waste time.

MILO: (yawning) I might as well. That's where I seem to be going anyway. Tell me, does everyone here do nothing?

LETHARGARIAN 3 AND LETHARGARIAN 4:   Everyone but the terrible watchdog.

LETHARGARIAN 5:   He's always sniffing around to see that nobody wastes time. A most unpleasant character.

MILO: The watchdog?

LETHARGARIAN 1: The watchdog!

NARRATOR 1: The Lethargarian fainted with fright, for racing down the road barking furiously and kicking up a great cloud of dust was the very dog of which they had been speaking.

LETHARGARIAN 2: Run!

LETHARGARIAN 3: Wake up!

LETHARGARIAN 4: Run!

LETHARGARIAN 5: Here he comes!

LETHARGARIAN 1: The watchdog!

NARRATOR 2: Great shouts filled the air as the Lethargarians scattered in all directions and soon disappeared entirely.

WATCHDOG: (puffing and panting) R-R-R-G-H-R-O-R-R-H-F-F.

NARRATOR 1: Milo's eyes opened wide, for there in front of him was a large dog with a perfectly normal head, four feet, and a tail—and the body of a loudly ticking alarm clock.

WATCHDOG: (growling) What are you doing here?

MILO: (apologetically) Just killing time, you see—

WATCHDOG: (roaring furiously) Killing time! It's bad enough wasting time without killing it. Why are you in the Doldrums anyway—don't you have anywhere to go?

MILO: I was on my way to Dictionopolis when I got stuck here. Can you help me?

NARRATOR 2: The dog replied, carefully winding himself with his left hind leg,

WATCHDOG: Help you! You must help yourself. I suppose you know why you got stuck.

MILO: I guess I just wasn't thinking.

NARRATOR 2: The dog's alarm went off and he shouted.

WATCHDOG: (shouting) Precisely! Now you know what you must do.

MILO: I'm afraid I don't.

WATCHDOG: (impatiently) Well, since you got here by not thinking, it seems reasonable to expect that, in order to get out, you must start thinking.

NARRATOR 1: And with that he hopped into the car.

WATCHDOG: Do you mind if I get in? I love automobile rides.

NARRATOR 2: Milo began to think as hard as he could (which was very difficult, since he wasn't used to it). He thought of

97

birds that swim and fish that fly. He thought of yester-day's lunch and tomorrow's dinner. He thought of words that begin with J and numbers that end in 3. And, as he thought, the wheels began to turn.

MILO: (happily) We're moving, we're moving!

WATCHDOG: (scolding) Keep thinking!

NARRATOR 1 AND NARRATOR 2:   The End.

The Knee-High Man

BY JULIUS LESTER

THE KNEE-HIGH MAN

Julius Lester has written some wonderful books for children and young adults. His *To Be a Slave* was a Newbery Medal Honor Book. "The Knee-High Man" is one of seven stories in a collection of short stories from American black folklore.

Although the story calls for a Mr. Horse, a Mr. Bull, and a Mr. Owl, all parts can be played by girls or boys. The knee-high man and the animals must all have distinctive personalities. Try to show your personality through your voice.

Players: 6

| Narrator 1 | Knee-High Man | Mr. Bull |
| Narrator 2 | Mr. Horse | Mr. Owl |

NARRATOR 1: I'm _____.
     I am a narrator.

NARRATOR 2: I'm _____.
     I am also a narrator.

KNEE-HIGH MAN: I'm _____.
     I play the knee-high man.

MR. HORSE: I'm _____.
     I play Mr. Horse.

MR. BULL: I'm _____.
     I play Mr. Bull.

MR. OWL: I'm _____.
     I play Mr. Owl.

NARRATOR 1:   Once upon a time there was a knee-high man. He was no taller than a person's knees. Because he was so short, he was very unhappy.

NARRATOR 2:   He wanted to be big like everybody else.

NARRATOR 1:   One day he decided to ask the biggest animal he could find how he could get big.

NARRATOR 2:   He went to see Mr. Horse.

KNEE-HIGH MAN: Mr. Horse, how can I get big like you?

MR. HORSE: Well, eat a whole lot of corn. Then run around a lot. After a while you'll be as big as me.

NARRATOR 1:   The knee-high man did just that. He ate so much corn that his stomach hurt.

KNEE-HIGH MAN: (groan and hold stomach)

NARRATOR 2:   Then he ran and ran and ran until his legs hurt. But he didn't get any bigger.

NARRATOR 1:   He decided that Mr. Horse had told him wrong. He decided to ask Mr. Bull.

KNEE-HIGH MAN: Mr. Bull, how can I get big like you?

MR. BULL: Eat a whole lot of grass. Then bellow as loud as you can. The first thing you know, you'll be big as me.

NARRATOR 2:   So the knee-high man ate a whole field of grass. That made his stomach hurt.

KNEE-HIGH MAN: (groan and hold stomach)

NARRATOR 1:   He bellowed and bellowed and bellowed all day and all night. That made his throat hurt.

NARRATOR 2:   But he didn't get any bigger. So he decided that Mr. Bull was all wrong too.

NARRATOR 1:   Now he didn't know anyone else to ask. One night he heard Mr. Owl hooting, and he remembered that Mr. Owl knew everything.

KNEE-HIGH MAN: Mr. Owl, how can I get big like Mr. Horse and Mr. Bull?

MR. OWL: What do you want to be big for?

KNEE-HIGH MAN: I want to be big so that when I get into a fight, I can whip everybody.

MR. OWL: (hooting) Anybody ever try to pick a fight with you?

NARRATOR 1:   The knee-high man thought a minute.

KNEE-HIGH MAN: Well, now that you mention it, nobody ever did try to start a fight with me.

MR. OWL: Well. You don't have any reason to fight. Therefore you don't have any reason to be bigger than you are.

KNEE-HIGH MAN: But Mr. Owl, I want to be big so I can see far into the distance.

MR. OWL.   (hooting) If you climb a tall tree, you can see into the distance from the top.

102

NARRATOR 2: The knee-high man was quiet for a minute.

KNEE-HIGH MAN: Well, I hadn't thought of that.

NARRATOR 1: Mr. Owl hooted again.

MR. OWL: And that's what's wrong, Mr. Knee-High Man. You hadn't done any thinking at all. I'm smaller than you, and you don't see me worrying about being big. Mr. Knee-High Man, you wanted something that you didn't need.

NARRATOR 2: The End.

Mirrors:
Two Poems for Three Voices

Readers: 3

YOU-TU
by Charlotte Pomerantz

READER 1: You are you,
Not me,
But you.
Look in the mirror
Peek-a-boo
The face that you see
Isn't me—
It's you.

READER 2: Tú eres tú.
No yo,
Pero tú.
Mira al espejo
Peek-a-boo
La cara que miras
No soy yo—
Eres tú.

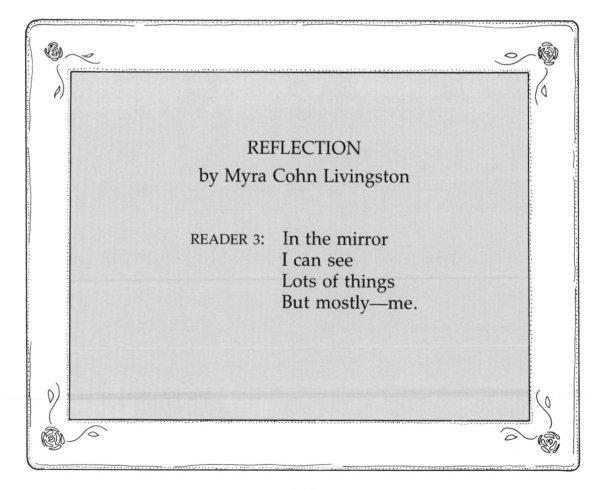

REFLECTION
by Myra Cohn Livingston

READER 3:   In the mirror
I can see
Lots of things
But mostly—me.

Down with President Stomach

DOWN WITH PRESIDENT STOMACH

The following play is adapted from a West African folktale. The characters may sit on the floor or on the edge of a desk while the narrator stands. As each character speaks he should perform the same mechanical action that his character dictates the entire time he is speaking and when his name is mentioned. This play requires more motion than many of the selections, so if you have a particularly active group, this is the perfect choice.

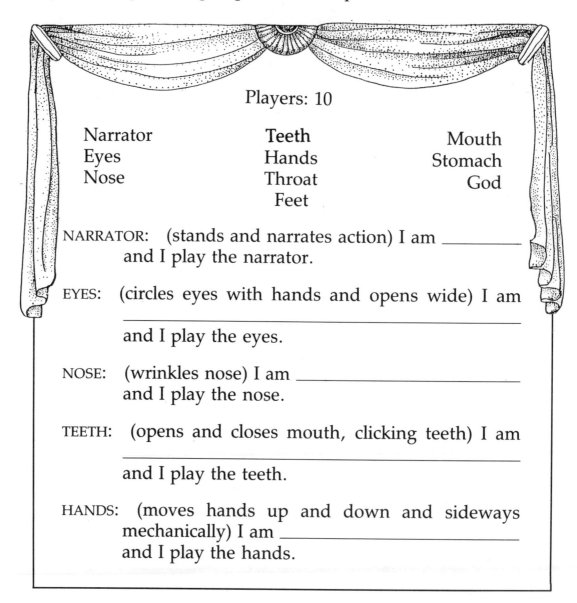

Players: 10

Narrator	**Teeth**	Mouth
Eyes	Hands	Stomach
Nose	Throat	God
	Feet	

NARRATOR: (stands and narrates action) I am _____ and I play the narrator.

EYES: (circles eyes with hands and opens wide) I am

_____

and I play the eyes.

NOSE: (wrinkles nose) I am _____ and I play the nose.

TEETH: (opens and closes mouth, clicking teeth) I am

_____

and I play the teeth.

HANDS: (moves hands up and down and sideways mechanically) I am _____ and I play the hands.

THROAT: (strokes throat) I am _____
and I play the throat.

FEET: (lifts feet up and down) I am _____
and I play the feet.

MOUTH: (circles hands around mouth) I am _____
and I play the mouth.

STOMACH: (sits up straight and pats stomach with
both hands) I am _____
and I play the stomach.

GOD: (speaks without moving; arms folded in front of
chest) I am _____
and I play God.

NARRATOR: God created man with feet, hands, eyes, nose, teeth, throat, mouth, and a stomach. God made the heart the Secretary and the stomach the President. Each part of the body had a particular job to perform.

EYES: We see.

NOSE: I smell.

TEETH: We chew.

HANDS: We hold, cut, and grab.

THROAT: I swallow.

FEET: We walk.

MOUTH: I hold.

STOMACH: I keep all the things that come into the body.

NARRATOR: Once the parts of the body began to feel jealous. They seemed to be working for Stomach and getting nothing in return.

THROAT: Listen, all the food that goes through me is gone in a minute. I think Stomach ties a rope around it and pulls it down for himself. Let's elect a new president and do away with Stomach.

TEETH: You're right. We chew the food, but Stomach is the one who takes it in and enjoys it by himself. You better vote against this president or I will leave and go to live in a foreign country.

EYES: You're in a better situation than we are. After all, at least, friend Throat, the food does pass through you; all we get to do is look.

NARRATOR: Now Feet wished to be heard.

FEET: We are also unhappy. We only walk to the food, but never get anything to eat.

HANDS: Let's go and talk to God. We will tell him that Stomach is greedy and makes a poor president.

ALL: Yes! Yes! Let's go.

NARRATOR: The body parts all agreed. A delegation was sent to God.

ALL (except Stomach): We are against President Stomach.

NARRATOR: God asked them if they knew what they were talking about.

GOD: Do you know what you are talking about?

NOSE: You made us. Yes, we know what we are talking about. We do not want Stomach for President. Look, he even looks like an overstuffed lady's handbag.

GOD: Say nothing that you will be sorry for in the future.

NARRATOR: God suggested that they return to their home to decide who they wanted for President. He cautioned them not to eat anything lest President Stomach keep using their work. They were happy.

MOUTH: Stomach thinks he is the only one created by God. We'll show him we don't need him.

THROAT: I'm glad God said we shouldn't feed him.

NARRATOR: God had promised to meet them in two days' time.

ALL (except Stomach), chanting: No! No! Down with President Stomach!

NARRATOR: On the morning of the third day the opposition had not eaten for two long days. Each part of the body was mighty hungry. They asked Left Eye to be President, but Left Eye said:

EYE: I cannot see very well today. I cannot be President.

NARRATOR: Then they asked Left Foot.

FOOT: Sorry, I cannot be President. I can hardly stand up today.

TEETH: I couldn't chew anything even if there was something to chew. I cannot be President.

NOSE: I haven't smelled anything for at least a day. I cannot be President.

HANDS: It is hard for me to hold, cut, or grab. I must decline any suggestion that I be President.

NARRATOR: They returned to God and explained that they had reconsidered. They wanted Stomach to be their leader since he could hold so much. Now they could see that Stomach had been fair dividing the food equally among them.

HANDS: Lord, we want Stomach to be our leader.

TEETH: Yes, we would like him for our king.

GOD: Hands, cook dinner and feed it to the Stomach. He shall be your king.

NARRATOR: Hands made supper and the body ate it. A short time later everyone was feeling better.

EYES: I can see again.

FEET: I can walk again.

THROAT: I feel better.

TEETH: I feel better.

NOSE: I can smell again.

MOUTH: Let us sing to our new leader.

ALL (except Stomach): Long live King Stomach! Long live King
Stomach!

STOMACH: (smiles and pats his stomach).

ALL: The End.

Jamboree

by David McCord

Readers: 10

ALL: "Jamboree" by David McCord

READER 1: A rhyme for ham?

ALL: Jam.

READER 2: A rhyme for mustard?

ALL: Custard.

READER 3: A rhyme for steak?

ALL: Cake.

READER 4: A rhyme for rice?

ALL: Another slice.

READER 5: A rhyme for stew?

ALL: You.

READER 6: A rhyme for mush?

ALL: Hush.

READER 7: A rhyme for prunes?

ALL: Goons.

READER 8: A rhyme for pie?

ALL: I.

READER 9: A rhyme for iced tea?

ALL: Me.

READER 10: For the pantry shelf?

ALL: Myself.

A Peanut Butter
Sandwich

from *The Mouse and the Motorcycle*
BY BEVERLY CLEARY

A PEANUT BUTTER SANDWICH

Beverly Cleary has been amusing children with her books for many years. You may have read her popular Henry Huggins or Ramona books. *The Mouse and the Motorcycle* and its sequel, *Ralph S. Mouse*, tell about the friendship between a boy and a mouse, and the fun they have together.

In this chapter, Keith, the boy who has come to stay at the Mountain View Inn with his parents, and Ralph, the mouse who lives in a knothole in Keith's room, have already become fast friends. They both love motorcycles and cars, and Keith has generously lent Ralph his little red motorcycle, which Ralph discovers is just his size!

Players: 4

Narrator   Keith   Ralph   Mother

NARRATOR: We would like to present a portion of *The Mouse and the Motorcycle* by Beverly Cleary. I am

_____

and I'm your narrator.

KEITH: I am _____
and I play Keith.

RALPH: I am _____
and I play Ralph.

MOTHER: I am _____
and I play Ralph's mother.

NARRATOR: As our story begins, Ralph has just returned home after a night spent exploring the hotel on Keith's little red motorcycle. Unfortunately, as he was speeding back into Keith's room, Keith's mother happened to catch a glimpse of him. Luckily, Keith was able to hide Ralph before his mother could be sure she had really seen a mouse, but it was a close call for Ralph!

KEITH: (scolding) I told you to be careful!

RALPH: It wasn't my fault the door blew shut.

KEITH: You didn't have to stay out so long.

RALPH: What's the use of having a motorcycle if you can't go tearing around staying out late?

KEITH: You don't have a motorcycle. I just let you use mine. And you'd better be careful. I like that motorcycle and I don't want anything to happen to it.

RALPH: (apologetically) I'll take care of it. I don't want anything to happen to it either.

KEITH: It's going to be harder to get a chance to ride it now that my mother has seen you. She's a terribly good housekeeper and she's sure to complain to the management.

RALPH: Speaking of breakfast, you people are too tidy. I'm not getting enough to eat around here. You don't leave any crumbs.

KEITH: (surprised) I never thought of it. What would you like?

NARRATOR: Ralph was astounded. This was the first time in his life anyone had asked him what he would like to eat. It

115

had always been a question of what he could get his paws on.

RALPH: (astonished) You mean I have a choice?

KEITH: Sure. All I have to do is order it when we go down to breakfast and then bring you some.

NARRATOR: Ralph had to take time to think. After a diet of graham crackers provided by little children, bits of candy and an occasional peanut or apple core left by medium-sized children, or a crust of toast and a dab of jam left by an adult who had ordered breakfast from room service, the possibilities of choosing his own meal were almost too much!

RALPH: I know what I'd like, but I don't know what you call it. Once some people who said they were almost out of money stayed in these rooms. They had four children, all of them hungry, and they couldn't afford to go to the dining room so they got some bread and spread it with something brown out of a jar and put some more bread on top of that. They whispered all the time they were eating, because they didn't want the maid or bellboy to know they were having a meal in their room. Afterwards they all got down on their hands and knees and picked up every single crumb on the carpet so no one would guess they had eaten in their rooms. It was a great disappointment.

KEITH: (laughing) It was a peanut butter sandwich. Sure, I'll bring you a peanut butter sandwich. Or part of one. It'll be kind of a funny breakfast, but I won't mind that.

RALPH: Where will you leave it?

KEITH: I'll tell you what, I'll poke it through the knothole.

RALPH: Just like room service! Uh—what about the motorcycle? Where are you going to leave that?

KEITH: In my suitcase, I guess.

RALPH: (pleading) Ah, come on. Have a heart. Leave it someplace where I can get it while you're out during the day.

KEITH: You're supposed to be in your mousehole asleep, not riding around in the daylight where people can see you.

RALPH: Well, can't a fellow even look at it? I bet you like to look at big motorcycles yourself.

KEITH: Yes, I do. Well—I'll leave it back under the bed like I said, but you promise not to ride it until after dark.

RALPH: Scout's honor!

NARRATOR: Ralph jumped off the bed and ran off to the knothole. Ralph's home was furnished with a clutter of things people drop on the floor of a hotel room—bits of Kleenex, hair, ravelings. His mother was always planning to straighten it out, but she never got around to it. She was always too busy fussing and worrying. Now, as Ralph expected, she was dividing Ry-Krisp crumbs among his squeaky bunch of little brothers and sisters while she waited to scold him.

MOTHER: Ralph, if I have told you once, I have told you a thousand times—

RALPH: Guess what! Somebody in 215 is going to bring us a real peanut butter sandwich!

117

MOTHER: (frightened) Ralph! You haven't been associating with *people!*

RALPH: Ah, he's just a boy. He wouldn't hurt us. He likes mice.

MOTHER: But he's a *person.*

RALPH: That doesn't mean he has to be bad. Just like Pop used to say, people shouldn't say all mice are timid just because some mice are. Or that all mice play when the cat's away just because some do.

MOTHER: Just the same, Ralph, I do wish you would be more careful whom you associate with. I am so afraid you'll fall in with the wrong sort of friends.

RALPH: I'm growing up. I'm getting too old to hang around a mouse nest all the time. I want to go out and see the world. I want to go down on the ground floor and see the kitchen and the dining room and the storeroom and the garbage cans out back.

MOTHER: Oh, Ralph! Not the ground floor. Not all the way down there. You aren't old enough.

RALPH: (stoutly) Yes, I am.

MOTHER: There's no telling what you might run into down there—mousetraps, cats, poison. Why, out by the garbage cans you might even be seen by an owl!

118

RALPH: I don't care. Someday I'm going downstairs.

MOTHER: (imploring) But think of the owls, Ralph. We moved into the hotel because of the owls. It was after your Uncle Leroy disappeared and his bones were found in an owl pellet.

NARRATOR: The mother mouse's plea was interrupted by the sound of Keith returning to room 215.

RALPH: Now you'll see.

KEITH: Psst! Here it is. The waitress thought I was crazy, ordering a peanut butter sandwich along with my cornflakes for breakfast, but here it is.

NARRATOR: He stuffed half a sandwich a bit at a time into the hole where Ralph seized the pieces and pulled them all the way through.

KEITH: Listen, we're going to be gone most of the day. The dining room is packing us a picnic lunch, and we're going to drive along some of the back roads and visit some old mining towns.

RALPH: Thanks a lot! Have fun.

KEITH: See you tonight. Have a good day's sleep.

NARRATOR: Ralph's mother could not help being impressed by the sight of that peanut butter sandwich.

MOTHER: Just like room service. Why, it's a peanut butter and *jelly* sandwich and it even has butter in it.

RALPH: (with his mouth full) I told you he would bring it!

NARRATOR: The End.

Mighty Mikko

BY PARKER FILLMORE

MIGHTY MIKKO

This Reader's Theater selection is an adaptation of a longer tale from *The Shepherd's Nosegay*. It may remind you of "Puss and Boots," which is a more familiar version of the same story.

This is a long play in which the plot and characters have a chance to develop more fully than in some of the shorter selections. Think about your character before you begin reading aloud. Are you the wily fox or modest Mikko or the lazy Worm? The audience plays an especially important role in this play, so it is the perfect choice for a group in which everyone wants to participate.

Players: 6+

Narrator	Mikko	Princess
Fox	King	Worm

Audience Participation

NARRATOR: I am _____.
    I play the narrator.

FOX: I am _____.
    I play the fox.

MIKKO: I am _____.
    I play Mikko.

KING: I am _____.
    I play the king.

PRINCESS: I am _____.
    I play the princess.

WORM: I am _____.
    I play The Worm.

Scene One

NARRATOR: Mikko was a lonely woodsman. When he found a fox in one of his traps he carefully released him and took him home. They became very good friends.

FOX: Mikko, why are you so sad?

MIKKO: Because I'm lonely.

FOX: You ought to get married! Then you wouldn't feel so lonely.

MIKKO: How can I get married? I can't marry a poor girl because I'm too poor myself, and a rich girl wouldn't marry me.

FOX: Nonsense. You're a fine man. What more could a princess ask?

MIKKO: A princess would never marry me.

FOX: I'm serious. How would you like to marry the princess of this country?

MIKKO: Any man would be happy to marry her.

FOX: Fine. I'll arrange the wedding for you.

Scene Two

NARRATOR: The fox went to see the king.

KING: Good morning. What can I do for you?

FOX: My master sends you greetings. He would like to borrow your bushel measure.

KING: My bushel measure? Who is your master and why does he want my bushel measure?

FOX: Surely you have heard of Mikko, haven't you? Mighty Mikko he is called.

NARRATOR: The king had never heard of Mighty Mikko, but he thought he should have heard of him.

KING: Ah yes. Mikko. Mighty Mikko. Yes. Yes, of course.

FOX: My master is about to start on a journey and he needs a bushel measure for a very particular reason.

NARRATOR: The king didn't understand, but he pretended that he did.

KING: Yes. Yes. I understand.

NARRATOR: The fox carried the bushel measure into the woods. He dug up a gold coin here and a gold coin there that had been hidden by people through the years. He stuck the coins into the cracks in the bushel measure.

FOX: Good morning, Your Majesty. I have come to thank you on behalf of my master Mighty Mikko for lending us the bushel measure.

NARRATOR: The king looked in the bushel measure to see what this Mighty Mikko had measured. He was surprised to see gold coins sticking in the cracks. He thought, "This Mighty Mikko must be very rich to be so careless with his wealth."

KING: I'm glad your master could find a good use for my bushel measure. I would like to meet your master. Won't you and he come and visit me?

NARRATOR: This was what the fox wanted the king to say, but he pretended to hesitate.

FOX: Thank you for your kind invitation. I'm sorry he won't be able to visit at this time. He is about to begin a long journey to inspect a number of foreign princesses.

NARRATOR: This made the king all the more anxious to have Mikko visit him at once. If Mikko should see his daughter he might fall in love with her and marry her before he saw any of the foreign princesses.

KING: My dear fellow. Please try to have your master visit before he starts out on his travels.

FOX: (looking embarrassed) I'm so sorry, sire. Excuse me for being so frank, but I'm afraid your castle is not big enough to house the immense retinue he travels with.

KING: My dear fox, I'll give you anything in the world if your master will come and visit at once.

FOX: Well, sometimes he does travel disguised as a poor woodsman, attended only by me.

KING: Oh, *wonderful*. Please have him visit disguised as a poor woodsman. I can let him use any of my fine clothes once he is here.

FOX: I fear Your Majesty's wardrobe doesn't contain the kind of clothes my master is accustomed to.

KING: Come along this minute. You can choose any clothes you like for your master.

NARRATOR: The king and the fox looked over all the king's clothes. The fox picked out the very best outfits and laid them aside for Mikko's visit.

Scene Three

NARRATOR: The next morning the princess looked out of the window and saw a young woodsman and a fox walking towards the palace.

PRINCESS: Father, look! That must be Mikko. I think I could fall in love with that young man even if he were only a woodsman.

NARRATOR: Mikko changed into the king's clothes and was presented to the princess and the court. The next day the fox met privately with the king.

FOX: Sire, my master is a man of few words and quick judgment. He would like to marry the princess.

KING: My dear fellow. That is impossible.

FOX: Don't make your decision today. I will come again tomorrow.

NARRATOR: The king spoke to the princess.

KING: This young man Mikko would like to marry you.

PRINCESS: How wonderful. I would like to marry him.

NARRATOR: Mikko and the princess were soon married.

FOX: You see, I said you would marry the princess.

MIKKO: Yes, but now that I am married what shall I do? I can't stay here forever.

FOX: Don't worry. I will arrange everything. Tell the king you would like him to come visit you at your castle.

MIKKO: Sire, please come and visit at my castle.

KING: I would love to, Mikko.

FOX: (whispering to Mikko) Now, I'll run on ahead and get things ready for you.

MIKKO: But where are you going?

FOX: A wicked old dragon lives in a gorgeous castle a few days' march from here. He is called The Worm. I think The Worm's castle would suit you.

MIKKO: No doubt that is true. But how will you get it away from The Worm?

FOX: Trust me. In a few days start out with the king and princess toward The Worm's castle. Ask anyone you meet whose men they are and don't be surprised at the answer.

Scene Four

NARRATOR: The fox went to all the workmen around The Worm's castle and told them that a great army was coming to destroy.

FOX: If you are asked say "We are Mighty Mikko's Men."

NARRATOR: We ask you, the audience, to be these workmen. Please say, "We are Mighty Mikko's Men." (pause and speak to the audience) Come on. If a fierce army was coming to get you you would speak louder and with more conviction. Whose men are you? (pause and say with the audience) "We are Mighty Mikko's Men!"

Scene Five

FOX: Oh good. There is The Worm's castle.

NARRATOR: The dragon was lying on a sofa in his living room. He was too lazy to get up and greet the fox.

FOX: Good day. You are The Worm, aren't you?

WORM: Yes. I am The Great Worm.

FOX: Oh, how terrible. Well. Just thought I would stop in and say goodbye.

WORM: What do you mean?

FOX: Surely you have heard about it. A great army is coming to destroy you and your castle.

NARRATOR: The Worm was frightened. He knew he was too lazy and fat to fight a war.

WORM: What should I do?

FOX: If I were you I would run and hide in the tool shed out in the back.

128

WORM: Thank you for the idea.

NARRATOR: The Worm hid in the small tool chest. The fox set it on fire and that was the end of the wicked Worm! The king, the princess, and their servants started towards The Worm's castle.

PRINCESS: Look, Father. There are many men working in the fields.

KING: Whose men are you?

NARRATOR: The men answered (motion to audience to chant with you) "We are Mighty Mikko's Men. We are Mighty Mikko's Men!"

PRINCESS: Look, Father. There are many men working in the woods.

NARRATOR: The men answered (motion to audience to chant with you) "We are Mighty Mikko's Men. We are Mighty Mikko's Men!"

PRINCESS: Look, Father. There are many men working with those horses.

KING: Whose men are you?

NARRATOR: The men answered (motion to audience to chant with you) "We are Mighty Mikko's Men. We are Mighty Mikko's Men!"

KING: Mikko certainly must be rich to have all these fields, this fine forest, and all those horses.

NARRATOR: Mikko stood at the castle door and received his guests.

MIKKO: Welcome, Father. Welcome, Wife. Welcome all of you.

KING: Your castle is so much grander than mine that I hesitate ever asking you back for a visit.

MIKKO: My dear Father-in-law, when I first entered your castle, I thought it was the most beautiful castle in the world.

KING: What a nice modest young man.

PRINCESS: I would love him even if he were a woodsman.

NARRATOR: The servants of the king and the servants of Mikko all shouted (motion to audience to chant with you) "We are Mighty Mikko's Men. We are Mighty Mikko's Men!"

PRINCESS: And we lived . . .

MIKKO: happily ever after.

NARRATOR: The End.

Fifteen Seconds

By Michael Rosen

Players: 2

Mom   Child

MOM: "Child"

CHILD: by Michael Rosen

MOM: Fifteen seconds
If you don't put your shoes on before I count
fifteen then we won't go to the woods to climb
the chestnut one

CHILD: But I can't find them

MOM: Two

CHILD: I can't

MOM: They're under the sofa three

CHILD: No

MOM: O yes
Four five six

CHILD: Stop—they've got knots they've got knots

MOM: You should untie the laces when you take your
shoes off seven

CHILD: Will you do one shoe while I do the other
then?

131

MOM: Eight but that would be cheating

CHILD: Please

MOM: All right

CHILD: It always . . .

MOM: Nine

CHILD: It always sticks—I'll use my teeth

MOM: Ten

CHILD: It won't it won't
It has—look.

MOM: Eleven

CHILD: I'm not wearing any socks

MOM: Twelve

CHILD: Stop counting stop counting. Mum where are
my socks mum

MOM: They're in your shoes. Where you left them.

CHILD: I didn't

MOM: Thirteen

CHILD: O they're inside out and upside down and
bundled up

MOM: Fourteen
Have you done the knot on the shoe you
were . . .

CHILD: Yes

MOM: Put it on the right foot

CHILD: But socks don't have right and wrong foot

MOM: The shoes silly
Fourteen and a half

CHILD: I am I am. Wait.
Don't go to the woods without me
Look that's one shoe already

MOM: Fourteen and threequarters

CHILD: There

MOM: You haven't tied the bows yet

CHILD: We could do them on the way there

MOM: No we won't fourteen and seven eighths

CHILD: Help me then
You know I'm not fast at bows

MOM: Fourteen and fifteen sixteeeenths

CHILD: A single bow is all right isn't it

MOM: Fifteen we're off

CHILD: See I did it.
Didn't I?

Learning

by Judith Viorst

Readers: 3

READER 2: "Learning" by Judith Viorst

READER 1: I'm learning to say thank you.

READER 2: And I'm learning to say please.

READER 3: And I'm learning to use Kleenex,
Not my sweater, when I sneeze.

READER 1: And I'm learning not to dribble.

READER 2: And I'm learning not to slurp.

READER 3: And I'm learning (though it sometimes really hurts me)
Not to burp.

READER 1: And I'm learning to chew softer
When I eat corn on the cob.

ALL: And I'm learning that it's much
Much easier to be a slob.

The Emperor's Prized Possession

THE EMPEROR'S PRIZED POSSESSION

This folktale makes fun of an emperor who takes himself very seriously. This emperor loved his pet cat more than anything else in the world. The prime minister and the emperor's family humor him because he is The Emperor. The voice of the cat as represented by the collective voice of the audience gives this play a charmingly nonsensical feel.

Players: 6 +

Narrator	Wife	Son
Emperor	Prime Minister	Daughter
	Audience Participants	

NARRATOR: My name is _____
and I play the narrator. We would like to tell you the story "The Emperor's Prized Possession."

EMPEROR: My name is _____
and I play the emperor.

WIFE: My name is _____
and I play the emperor's wife.

PRIME MINISTER: My name is _____
and I play the prime minister.

SON: My name is _____
and I play the emperor's son.

DAUGHTER: My name is _____
and I play the emperor's daughter.

NARRATOR: The most important player in our story is the cat. We would like you, the audience, to play the emperor's cat. When the cat speaks, please say "Meow." Let's practice. Everyone say "Meow." Good. Try it again. And now for our story. There was once an emperor.

EMPEROR: I love my cat. I love my cat more than anything else in the whole world.

NARRATOR: And the cat said . . . (motion to audience to meow).

EMPEROR: I don't know what to call my cat. She should have a very important-sounding name. The most powerful thing in the universe is the sky because it covers the whole world. I shall call my cat "Sky." Cat, you are now Sky.

NARRATOR: And the cat said . . . (motion to audience to meow).

WIFE: Husband, you are making a mistake. The sky is not all-powerful. Look up above. There is a cloud covering the sky.

EMPEROR: You are right. A cloud can cover the sky and hide it. From now on I will call my lovely cat "Cloud." Cat, you are now Cloud.

NARRATOR: And the cat said . . . (motion to audience to meow).

PRIME MINISTER: Excuse me, sire. We have been calling your cat Cloud for two weeks, but I think you have made a mistake. Look at the clouds. They are being pushed and moved by the wind. The wind is much more powerful than a cloud.

EMPEROR: You are right. The wind is much more powerful than any cloud. From now on everyone must call my cat "Wind." Cat, you are now Wind.

NARRATOR: And the cat said . . . (motion audience to meow).

SON: Excuse me, Father. We have been calling your cat Wind for three weeks, but I think you are making a mistake. Look at the wall around the palace. The wall is stopping the wind.

EMPEROR: You are right. The wall will not let the wind come through. The wall must be more important than the wind. From now on we will call my cat "Wall." Cat, you are now Wall.

NARRATOR: And the cat said . . . (motion audience to meow).

DAUGHTER: Excuse me, Father. We have been calling your cat Wall for three weeks, but I think you are making a mistake. Look at that mouse. It is chewing a hole right through the wall.

EMPEROR: You are right. The mouse is more powerful than the wall. From this moment on everyone must call my cat "Mouse." Cat, you are now Mouse.

NARRATOR: And the cat said . . . (motion audience to meow).

WIFE: Husband, I think you have made a terrible mistake. Look, your cat is chasing the mouse.

EMPEROR: You are right. Clearly, my cat is the most powerful animal or thing in the whole world. From now on everyone will call my cat . . . Cat.

NARRATOR: And from that moment on, cat was called Cat. And the cat said . . . (motion audience to meow).
The End.

ADMIT ONE

THE EMPEROR'S PRIZED POSSESSION

Banjo Tune

by William Jay Smith

Children love to supply the refrain to this infectious poem. The reader should cue the audience to chime in with "plunk-a-plunk" with a hand motion or simply by pausing expectantly and looking toward the audience.

READER: Plunk-a-Plunk! Plunk-a-Plunk!
  I sit in the attic on an old trunk.

AUDIENCE: Plunk-a-Plunk!

READER: Locked in the old trunk is my wife,
  And she may be there for the rest of her life.

AUDIENCE: Plunk-a-Plunk!

READER: She screams, "Let me out of here, you fool!"
  I say, "I will when your soup gets cool."

AUDIENCE: Plunk-a-Plunk!

READER: She screams, "Let me out or I'll bean you, brother!"
  I say, "Now, come on, tell me another!"

AUDIENCE: Plunk-a-Plunk!

READER: To keep one's wife in a trunk is wrong,
  But I keep mine there for the sake of my song.

AUDIENCE: Plunk-a-Plunk!

READER: My song is hokum, my song is bunk,
  And there's just a wad of old clothes in this trunk:
  Not even the junkman would want this junk!

AUDIENCE: Plunk-a-Plunk!
  Plunk-a-Plunk!
  Plunk!

What Is Purple?

by Mary O'Neill

Readers: 5

ALL: "What Is Purple" by Mary O'Neill

READER 1:   Time is purple
Just before night
When most people
Turn on the light—

READER 2:   But if you don't it's
A beautiful sight.

READER 3:   Asters are purple,

READER 4:   There's purple ink.

READER 5:   Purple's more popular
Than you think . . .

READER 1:   It's sort of a great
Grandmother to pink.

READER 2:   There are purple shadows

READER 3:   And purple veils,

READER 4:   Some ladies purple
Their fingernails.

READER 5:   There's purple jam

READER 1:   And purple jell

READER 2:   And a purple bruise
Next day will tell
Where you landed
When you fell.

READER 3:   The purple feeling
Is rather put-out

READER 4:   The purple look is a
Definite pout.

READER 5:   But the purple sound
Is the loveliest thing

ALL: It's a violet opening
In the spring.

How the Camel Got His Hump

BY RUDYARD KIPLING

HOW THE CAMEL GOT HIS HUMP

Rudyard Kipling wrote many adventure stories. You may have read *The Jungle Book* or *Kim*, two especially popular books. He also wrote a collection of "Pourquoi" or "Why" stories. Some favorites are "The Elephant's Child," which tells how the elephant got his trunk; "How the Leopard Got His Spots"; and "How the Whale Got His Throat."

I have included "How the Camel Got His Hump" almost exactly as Rudyard Kipling wrote it. Some of the sentences are long and may require practice, and there are some words you may not know but should be able to figure out from the context of the story.

Each of the players, including the narrators, has a distinct personality. Before you begin, think about what sort of personality your character has.

Players: 8

| Narrator 1 | Camel | Dog | Man |
| Narrator 2 | Horse | Ox | Djinn |

NARRATOR 1: I am _____
and I am one of the narrators.

NARRATOR 2: I am _____
and I am also a narrator.

CAMEL: I am _____.
I play the camel.

HORSE: I am _____.
I play the horse.

```
DOG:   I am _____
          I play the dog.

OX:   I am _____.
          I play the ox.

MAN:   I am _____.
          I play the man.

DJINN:   I am _____.
          I play the djinn.
```

NARRATOR 2:   We would like to present "How the Camel Got His Hump" by Rudyard Kipling.

NARRATOR 1:   (grandly, in sonorous tones) In the beginning of years, when the world was so new-and-all, and the animals were just beginning to work for man, there was a camel. He lived in the middle of a howling desert because he did not want to work; besides, he was a howler himself.

NARRATOR 2:   So he ate sticks and thorns and tamarisks and milkweed and prickles, most 'scruciating idle. When anybody spoke to him he said,

CAMEL: Humph!

NARRATOR 2:   Just,

CAMEL: Humph!

NARRATOR 2:   and no more.

NARRATOR 1:   Presently the horse came to him on Monday morning, with a saddle on his back and a bit in his mouth.

HORSE: Camel, O Camel, come out and trot like the rest of us.

CAMEL: Humph!

NARRATOR 1:   And the horse went away and told the man.

NARRATOR 2:   Presently the dog came to him with a stick in his mouth.

DOG: Camel, O Camel, come and fetch and carry like the rest of us.

CAMEL: Humph!

NARRATOR 2:   And the dog went away and told the man.

NARRATOR 1:   Presently the ox came to him, with the yoke on his neck.

OX: Camel, O Camel, come and plough like the rest of us.

CAMEL: Humph!

NARRATOR 1:   And the ox went away and told the man.

NARRATOR 2:   At the end of the day the man called the horse and the dog and the ox together.

MAN: Three, O three, I'm very sorry for you (with the world so new-and-all); but that humph-thing in the desert can't work, or he would have been here by now. I'm going to leave him alone, and you must work doubletime to make up for it.

NARRATOR 1:   That made the three very angry (with the world so new-and-all), and they held a palaver, and an *indaba*, and a *punchayet*, and a pow-wow on the edge of the desert; and the camel came chewing milkweed *most* 'scruciating idle, and laughed at them.

NARRATOR 2:   Then he said,

CAMEL: Humph!

NARRATOR 2:   and went away again.

NARRATOR 1:   Presently there came along the djinn in charge of all deserts, rolling on a cloud of dust (djinns always travel that way because it is magic), and he stopped to palaver and pow-wow with the three.

HORSE: Djinn of All Deserts: Is it right for anyone to be idle, with the world so new-and-all?

DJINN: (firmly) Certainly not.

HORSE: Well, there's a thing in the middle of your howling desert (and he's a howler himself) with a long neck and long legs, and he hasn't done a stroke of work since Monday morning. He won't trot.

DJINN: (whistling) Whew! That's my camel, for all the gold in Arabia! What does he say about it?

147

DOG: He says "Humph!" and he won't fetch and carry.

DJINN: Does he say anything else?

OX: Only "Humph!" and he won't plow.

DJINN: Very good. I'll "humph" him if you will kindly wait a minute.

NARRATOR 1:   The djinn rolled himself up in his dust cloak, and took a bearing across the desert, and found the camel most 'scruciatingly idle, looking at his own reflection in a pool of water.

DJINN: My long and bubbling friend: What's this I hear of your doing no work, with the world so new-and-all?

CAMEL: Humph!

NARRATOR 2:   The djinn sat down, with his chin in his hand, and began to think a great magic, while the camel looked at his own reflection in the pool of water.

DJINN: You've given the three extra work ever since Monday morning, all on account of your 'scruciating idleness.

NARRATOR 1:   The djinn went on thinking magics, with his chin in his hand.

CAMEL: Humph!

DJINN: I shouldn't say that again if I were you. You might say it once too often. Bubbles, I want you to work.

CAMEL: Humph!

NARRATOR 2:   No sooner had the camel said,

CAMEL: Humph!

NARRATOR 2:   than he saw his back, that he was so proud of, puffing up and puffing up into a great big lolloping humph.

DJINN: Do you see that? That's your very own humph that you've brought upon your very own self by not working. Today is Thursday, and you've done no work since Monday, when the work began. Now you are going to work.

CAMEL: (whining) How can I with this humph on my back?

DJINN: That's made a-purpose, all because you missed those three days. You will be able to work now for three days without eating, because you can live on your humph. Don't you ever say I never did anything for you. Come out of the desert and go to the three, and behave. Humph yourself!

NARRATOR 1:   And the camel humphed himself, humph and all, and went away to join the three. And from that day to this the camel always wears a humph (we call it "hump" now, not to hurt his feelings).

NARRATOR 2: But he has never yet caught up with the three days that he missed at the beginning of the world, and he has never yet learned how to behave.

ALL: Humph!

The Three Sillies

BY JOSEPH JACOBS

THE THREE SILLIES

Joseph Jacobs collected many folk and fairytales from the British Isles. You are certain to know some of them, such as "The Story of the Three Little Pigs," "The Story of the Three Bears," and "Jack the Giant Killer." "The Three Sillies" must be one of the earliest nonsense stories. Since the play is divided into four scenes, all the players do not have to remain "on stage" throughout the entire reading.

Players: 9

Narrator 1	Mother	Woman
Narrator 2	Father	Traveler
Girl	Gentleman	Villager

NARRATOR 1: My name is _____
and I play one of the narrators.

NARRATOR 2: My name is _____
and I also play a narrator.

GIRL: My name is _____
and I play the girl.

MOTHER: My name is _____
and I play the mother.

FATHER: My name is _____
and I play the father.

GENTLEMAN: My name is _____
and I play the gentleman.

WOMAN: My name is
and I play the woman.

TRAVELER: My name is _____
and I play the traveler.

VILLAGER: My name is _____
and I play the villager.

Scene One

NARRATOR 1: Once upon a time there was a farmer and his wife. They had one daughter who was being courted by a gentleman.

NARRATOR 2: Every evening he used to come to see her, and he would stop to supper at the farmhouse. The daughter would be sent down to the cellar to draw beer for supper.

NARRATOR 1: One evening she went down the stairs to draw the beer and she looked up at the ceiling and saw a mallet stuck in one of the beams.

NARRATOR 2: The girl began to think how dangerous it was to have the mallet there.

GIRL: Suppose him and me was to be married, and we was to have a son, and he was to grow up to be a man. Suppose he come down to the cellar to draw beer, like I'm doing now, and the mallet would fall on his head and kill him. What a dreadful thing that would be!

NARRATOR 1:   The girl put down her candle and jug and began a-crying.

GIRL: (starts to cry)

NARRATOR 2:   Well, they began to wonder upstairs why it took so long to get the beer. Her mother went down the stairs to find her daughter.

MOTHER: Whatever is the matter?

GIRL: Oh Mother! Look at that horrid mallet. Suppose we was to be married, and was to have a son, and he was to grow up, and was to come down to the cellar to draw the beer and the mallet was to fall on his head and kill him. What a dreadful thing that would be!

MOTHER: Dear, dear! What a dreadful thing that would be!

NARRATOR 1:   The mother sat next to the daughter and she too started to cry.

GIRL AND MOTHER: (cry)

NARRATOR 2:   Then after a bit the father began to wonder why they didn't come back and he went down to the cellar. He sees his wife and daughter sitting there a-crying and the beer all over the floor.

FATHER: Whatever is the matter?

MOTHER: Why, look at that horrid mallet. Just suppose, if our daughter and her sweetheart was to be married, and was to have a son, and he was to grow up, and was to come down into the cellar to draw the beer, and the mallet was to fall on his head and kill him, what a dreadful thing that would be.

FATHER: Dear, dear, dear! So it would!

NARRATOR 1: He sat down aside the other two and started a-crying.

GIRL, MOTHER, AND FATHER: (cry)

NARRATOR 2: Now the gentleman got tired of stopping up in the kitchen by himself, and at last he went down into the cellar too. The three they sat there a-crying side by side and the beer running all over the floor. He ran and turned off the beer tap.

GENTLEMAN: Whatever are you three doing, sitting there crying, and letting the beer run over the floor?

FATHER: Oh, look at that horrid mallet. Just suppose, if our daughter and her sweetheart was to be married, and was to have a son, and he was to grow up, and was to come down into the cellar to draw the beer, and the mallet was to fall on his head and kill him!

NARRATOR 1: Then they all started a-crying worse than before.

GIRL, MOTHER, AND FATHER: (cry)

NARRATOR 2: But the gentleman burst out a-laughing, and reached up and pulled out the mallet, and then he said,

155

GENTLEMAN: I've traveled many miles, and I never met three such big sillies as you three before. Now I shall start out on my travels again. When I can find three bigger sillies than you three, then I'll come back and marry your daughter.

NARRATOR 1:   So he wished them good-bye, and started off on his travels, and left them all crying because the girl had lost her sweetheart.

Scene Two

NARRATOR 2:   Well, he set out, and he traveled a long way, and at last he came to a woman's cottage that had some grass growing on the roof.

NARRATOR 1:   The woman was trying to get her cow to go up a ladder to the grass, and the poor thing wouldn't go.

GENTLEMAN: Whatever are you doing?

WOMAN: Why, look ye at all that beautiful grass. I'm going to get the cow on the roof to eat it.

GENTLEMAN: Oh, you poor silly! You should cut the grass and throw it down to the cow. You are one big silly.

Scene Three

NARRATOR 2:   The gentleman went on and on. He found an inn to stay the night. The inn was so full he had to share a room with another traveler.

156

NARRATOR 1:   The two men got along splendidly. In the morning the gentleman was surprised to see the traveler hang his trousers on the knob of the chest of drawers and run across the room and try to jump into them. He tried over and over again.

GENTLEMAN: Whatever are you doing?

TRAVELER: Oh dear. I do think trousers are the most awkward kind of clothes. I can't think who could have invented such things. It takes me a better part of an hour to get into mine every morning and I get so hot! How do you manage yours?

GENTLEMAN: Oh my! Let me show you how to do it. You are another big silly.

NARRATOR 2:   The gentleman showed the traveler how to put on his trousers and went on his travels again.

Scene Four

NARRATOR 1:   He came to a village and outside the village was a pond. Standing next to the pond was a man holding a rake.

GENTLEMAN: Whatever are you doing?

VILLAGER: Oh sir. The moon has fallen into the water and I'm trying to rake it out.

GENTLEMAN: Oh my. The moon hasn't fallen into the water. That's only the shadow. You are a big silly.

NARRATOR 2: Well, the gentleman had found three sillies who were sillier than the three sillies at home.

NARRATOR 1: So, the gentleman went back to the farmer's daughter. And if they didn't live happily forever after, that's nothing to do with you or me.

NARRATOR 1 AND NARRATOR 2: The End.

A Good Buy

A GOOD BUY

Throughout the Middle East, folk stories about foolish/wise characters abound. In Turkey, the Hodja stories are popular. Similar jokes and vignettes are told featuring the Goya from the Arabian peninsula. This play calls for five players (including the donkey). More can be added if you would like to hold a more lively auction.

Players: 5

Narrator   Donkey
Wife   Auctioneer
Goya

NARRATOR: I am _____ .
        I play the narrator.

WIFE: I am _____ .
        I play the wife.

GOYA: I am _____ .
        I play the Goya.

DONKEY: I am _____ .
        I play the donkey.

AUCTIONEER: I am _____ .
        I play the auctioneer.

NARRATOR: The Goya's donkey was old and stubborn.

WIFE: Husband, take that donkey to market and sell him. Buy a new one.

GOYA: A good idea, Wife. Come, donkey.

DONKEY: Hee haw.

NARRATOR: The Goya walked down the road thinking about his faithful donkey.

GOYA: Even though you are old and lazy, you've been a good friend.

DONKEY: Hee haw.

NARRATOR: The donkey auction was being held at the market-place. Reluctantly, the Goya handed over his donkey to the auctioneer.

GOYA: Here is my donkey, a faithful friend. Please sell him for me.

AUCTIONEER: But of course. A fine donkey like this should fetch a handsome price.

GOYA: Goodbye, old friend.

DONKEY: Hee haw.

NARRATOR: The auction was about to begin. Goya moved up front to get the best view.

161

AUCTIONEER: Step right up, folks. Here is a fine selection of donkeys.

NARRATOR: The Goya watched as the auctioneer led several donkeys into the circle.

AUCTIONEER: Friends, today we have an exceptionally fine collection of donkeys to tempt you.

NARRATOR: The Goya was astonished when his own donkey was led to the center of the circle.

DONKEY: Hee haw.

AUCTIONEER: Here we have a particularly fine animal. Look at the strong legs.

GOYA: That's true. My donkey does have strong legs.

AUCTIONEER: Look at the soft grey color. How this donkey glows!

GOYA: It does have a lovely coloring.

AUCTIONEER: Notice the lively look in this donkey's eyes.

GOYA: He does seem to have an eager look in his eyes.

AUCTIONEER: Have you ever seen such straight ears, such a luxurious tail?

GOYA: This donkey really does have perky ears. And that tail would surely be able to swat away flies.

AUCTIONEER: How much am I bid for this strong, capable animal?

NARRATOR: The Goya could hardly contain himself.

GOYA: (shouting) Five rials for that donkey!

NARRATOR: Someone else called out six rials.

GOYA: (excited) Ten! I'll buy him for ten!

AUCTIONEER: Sold to the Goya!

GOYA: What a fine buy I've made!

DONKEY: Hee haw.

NARRATOR: The Goya led his donkey home, happy to own such a useful, strong animal.

GOYA: Won't my wife be surprised that I have bought such a healthy donkey!

NARRATOR: The Goya's wife was indeed surprised to see the Goya leading his own donkey back to the house.

GOYA: Look, Wife. Here is our new donkey.

WIFE: Oh Goya, you must be fooling.

GOYA: But no. I paid ten rials for this magnificent animal.

WIFE: Oh no! You bought our own donkey back.

GOYA: But aren't you glad? He has been a good and faithful friend.

WIFE: But stubborn and lazy. Oh well. Welcome home, old friend.

DONKEY: Hee haw. Hee haw.

NARRATOR: The End.

Hershele
Gets a Meal

HERSHELE GETS A MEAL

Many stories are told about Hershele Ostropoler, a Jewish folk character. In this piece, Hershele should be solemn and determined until the very last line.

Players: 4

Narrator   Innkeeper
Hershele   Innkeeper's Wife

NARRATOR: My name is _____
            and I play the narrator.

HERSHELE: My name is _____
            and I play Hershele.

INNKEEPER: My name is _____
            and I play the innkeeper.

INNKEEPER'S WIFE: My name is _____
            and I play the innkeeper's wife.

NARRATOR: Hershele Ostropoler came to an inn.

HERSHELE: I would like some dinner, please.

INNKEEPER: Sorry. Our dinner service is over.

HERSHELE: What! I am very hungry.

166

INNKEEPER'S WIFE: Sorry, sir. The food has been put away for the night.

HERSHELE: But if I don't get any dinner I will have to do what my father did when he was hungry!

INNKEEPER: What did he do?

HERSHELE: (somberly) He did what he had to do.

NARRATOR: The innkeeper and his wife were frightened.

WIFE: Husband, what do you think his father did when he was hungry?

INNKEEPER: I don't know, Wife, but I don't want to find out. Quick, go get him some food!

NARRATOR: The wife returned with a steaming platter of food.

HERSHELE: This looks good.

NARRATOR: Hershele ate everything from the plate.

HERSHELE: That was very good. Thank you.

INNKEEPER: Before you go, sir, please tell us what your father did when he was hungry.

HERSHELE: (cheerfully) Why, certainly. When my father was hungry and couldn't get any food, he went to bed hungry.

NARRATOR: The End.

Ruby

BY FLORENCE PARRY HEIDE

RUBY

Tales for the Perfect Child is a wonderful collection of vignettes about children who are probably very much like children you know. In fact, in "Ruby," the tale I've chosen, you may recognize several people. If you have a baby brother, he is probably a lot like Clyde!

There are four parts in this play, including the character of Clyde, which is the perfect part for someone who wishes to participate but prefers not to speak.

Players: 4

Narrator   Ruby's mother
Ruby   Clyde, Ruby's baby brother

NARRATOR: I am _____
    and I play the narrator.

RUBY: I am _____
    and I play Ruby.

MOTHER: I am _____
    and I play Ruby's mother.

CLYDE: I am _____
    and I play Clyde, Ruby's baby brother.

NARRATOR: Ruby wanted to go over to Ethel's house to play.

MOTHER: No, Ruby. You must watch Clyde.

NARRATOR: Clyde was Ruby's baby brother. He had just learned to walk.

RUBY: I don't want to watch Clyde. I want to go over to Ethel's house to play.

NARRATOR: Ruby's mother was tired. She had been watching Clyde all day.

MOTHER: You have to watch Clyde because I have to take a bubble bath.

NARRATOR: Ruby's mother went into the bathroom. Ruby picked up the telephone to call Ethel.

RUBY: (dials Ethel's telephone number) I'll be over in a minute.

NARRATOR: Then Ruby watched Clyde. She watched him take all of the clothes out of all of the drawers in all of the bureaus in all of the rooms.

CLYDE: (takes everything out of all the drawers!)

NARRATOR: She watched him take all of the rice and all of the flour and all of the salt and all of the sugar and all of the coffee out of all of the kitchen cupboards and spill it all on the nice clean floor.

CLYDE: (spills everything in the kitchen!)

NARRATOR: She watched him pull the tablecloth off the kitchen table. The bananas that had been on the table landed on Clyde's head.

CLYDE: (pulls the tablecloth off the table and falls down!)

NARRATOR: Ruby watched Clyde start to cry very loudly.

CLYDE: (begins crying very loudly!)

NARRATOR: Ruby's mother came out of the bathroom.

MOTHER: What's going on? I told you to watch Clyde.

RUBY: (very seriously) I was watching him. I was watching him the whole time.

NARRATOR: In a few minutes Ruby was ringing Ethel's doorbell.

RUBY: (grinning) I told you I'd be over in a minute. I just had to watch Clyde.

NARRATOR: The End.

172

In Which Tigger Comes to the Forest and Has Breakfast

from *The House at Pooh Corner*

BY A. A. MILNE

IN WHICH TIGGER COMES TO THE FOREST
AND HAS BREAKFAST

Of all A. A. Milne's books for children, the best loved must be his stories about Christopher Robin and Pooh, the boy and the bear who "wherever they go, and whatever happens to them on the way, in that enchanted place at the top of the Forest . . . will always be playing."

In this selection from *The House at Pooh Corner*, Winnie-the-Pooh meets Tigger, an important character in many of the Pooh stories, for the very first time. Their adventures in search of something that Tiggers like to eat are told with great amusement and delight. This is the perfect Reader's Theater choice for an older group to perform for a younger group because, although children and adults of all ages enjoy Pooh and his companions, the slightly more sophisticated language is best suited to older readers.

Players: 8

Narrator   Tigger   Eeyore   Roo
Pooh   Piglet   Christopher Robin   Kanga

NARRATOR: My name is _____
           and I play the narrator.

POOH: My name is _____
       and I play Pooh.

TIGGER: My name is _____
         and I play Tigger.

PIGLET: My name is _____
          and I play Piglet.

EEYORE: My name is _____
          and I play Eeyore.

ROO: My name is _____
       and I play Roo.

CHRISTOPHER ROBIN: My name is _____
                     and I play Christopher Robin.

KANGA: My name is _____
         and I play Kanga.

NARRATOR: Welcome to our presentation from *The House at Pooh Corner* by A. A. Milne. Winnie-the-Pooh woke up suddenly in the middle of the night and listened. Then he got out of bed, lit his candle, and stumped across the room to see if anybody was trying to get into his honey-cupboard. They weren't, so he stumped back again, blew out his candle, and got into bed. Then he heard the noise again.

POOH: Is that you, Piglet?

NARRATOR: But it wasn't.

POOH: Come in, Christopher Robin.

NARRATOR: But Christopher Robin didn't.

POOH: (sleepily) Tell me about it tomorrow, Eeyore.

NARRATOR: But the noise went on. *"Worraworraworraworraworra,"* said Whatever-It-Was, and Pooh found that he wasn't asleep after all.

POOH: What can it be? There are lots of noises in the forest, but this is a different one. It isn't a growl, and it isn't a purr, and it isn't a bark, and it isn't the noise-you-make-before-beginning-a-piece-of-poetry, but it's a noise of some kind, made by a strange animal. And he's making it outside my door. So I shall get up and ask him not to do it.

NARRATOR: He got out of bed and opened his front door.

POOH: Hallo!

TIGGER: Hallo!

POOH: Oh! Hallo!

TIGGER: Hallo!

POOH: Oh, *there* you are! Hallo!

TIGGER: Hallo!

NARRATOR: Pooh was just going to say "Hallo" for the fourth time when he thought that he wouldn't, so he said: "Who is it?" instead.

POOH: Who is it?

TIGGER: Me.

POOH: Oh! Well, come here.

NARRATOR: So Tigger came here, and in the light of the candle he and Pooh looked at each other.

POOH: I'm Pooh.

TIGGER: I'm Tigger.

POOH: Oh!

NARRATOR: Pooh had never seen an animal like this before.

POOH: Does Christopher Robin know about you?

TIGGER: Of course he does.

POOH: Well, it's the middle of the night, which is a good time for going to sleep. And tomorrow morning we'll have some honey for breakfast. Do Tiggers like honey?

TIGGER: (cheerfully) They like everything.

POOH: Then if they like going to sleep on the floor, I'll go back to bed, and we'll do things in the morning. Good night.

NARRATOR: And Pooh got back into bed and went fast asleep. When he awoke in the morning, the first thing he saw was Tigger, sitting in front of the glass and looking at himself.

POOH: Hallo!

TIGGER: Hallo! I've found somebody just like me. I thought I was the only one of them.

NARRATOR: Pooh got out of bed, and began to explain what a looking-glass was, but just as he was getting to the interesting part, Tigger said,

TIGGER: Excuse me a moment, but there's something climbing up your table.

NARRATOR: And with one loud *Worraworraworraworraworra* he jumped at the end of the tablecloth, pulled it to the ground, wrapped himself up in it three times, rolled to the other end of the room, and, after a terrible struggle, got his head into the daylight again, and said cheerfully,

TIGGER: Have I won?

POOH: That's my tablecloth.

TIGGER: I wondered what it was.

POOH: It goes on the table and you put things on it.

TIGGER: Then why did it try to bite me when I wasn't looking?

POOH: I don't *think* it did.

TIGGER: It tried, but I was too quick for it.

NARRATOR: Pooh put the cloth back on the table, and he put a large honeypot on the cloth, and they sat down to breakfast. And as soon as they sat down, Tigger took a large mouthful of honey . . . and he looked up at the ceiling with his head on one side, and made exploring noises with his tongue, and considering noises, and what-have-we-got-here noises . . . and then he said in a very decided voice,

TIGGER: Tiggers don't like honey.

POOH: (trying to sound sad and regretful) Oh! I thought they liked everything.

TIGGER: Everything except honey.

NARRATOR: Pooh felt rather pleased about this, and said that as soon as he had finished his own breakfast, he would take Tigger round to Piglet's house, and Tigger could try some of Piglet's haycorns.

TIGGER: Thank you, Pooh, because haycorns is really what Tiggers like best.

NARRATOR: So after breakfast they went round to see Piglet, and Pooh explained as they went that Piglet was a Very Small Animal who didn't like bouncing, and asked Tigger not to be too Bouncy just at first. And Tigger, who had been hiding behind trees and jumping out on Pooh's shadow when it wasn't looking, said that Tiggers were only bouncy before breakfast, and that as soon as they had had a few haycorns they became Quiet and Refined. So by and by they knocked at the door of Piglet's house.

PIGLET: Hallo, Pooh.

POOH: Hallo, Piglet. This is Tigger.

PIGLET: (edging round to the other side of the table) Oh, is it? I thought Tiggers were smaller than that.

TIGGER: Not the big ones.

POOH: They like haycorns, so that's what we've come for, because poor Tigger hasn't had any breakfast yet.

NARRATOR: Piglet pushed the bowl of haycorns towards Tigger and said,

PIGLET: Help yourself.

NARRATOR: Then Piglet got close to Pooh and felt much braver, and said,

PIGLET: So you're Tigger? Well, well!

NARRATOR: But Tigger said nothing because his mouth was full of haycorns.

TIGGER: (still munching) Ee-ers o i a-ors.

POOH AND PIGLET: What?

TIGGER: Skoos ee.

NARRATOR: Tigger went outside for a moment, and when he came back he said firmly,

TIGGER: Tiggers don't like haycorns.

POOH: But you said they liked everything except honey.

TIGGER: Everything except honey and haycorns.

POOH: Oh, I see!

PIGLET: (happily) What about thistles?

TIGGER: Thistles is what Tiggers like best.

PIGLET: Then let's go along and see Eeyore.

NARRATOR: So the three of them went; and after they had walked and walked and walked, they came to the part of the forest where Eeyore was.

POOH: Hallo, Eeyore! This is Tigger.

EEYORE: What is?

POOH AND PIGLET: This.

NARRATOR: Tigger smiled his happiest smile and said nothing.

TIGGER: (smile)

NARRATOR: Eeyore walked all round Tigger one way, and then turned and walked all round him the other way.

EEYORE: What did you say it was?

POOH: Tigger.

EEYORE: Ah!

PIGLET: He's just come.

EEYORE: Ah!

TIGGER: (after thinking for a long time) When is he going?

NARRATOR: Pooh explained to Eeyore that Tigger was a great friend of Christopher Robin's, who had come to stay in the forest, and Piglet explained to Tigger that he mustn't

181

mind what Eeyore said because he was *always* gloomy; and Eeyore explained to Piglet that, on the contrary, he was feeling particularly cheerful this morning; and Tigger explained to anybody who was listening that he hadn't had any breakfast yet.

POOH: I knew there was something. Tiggers always eat thistles, so that was why we came to see you, Eeyore.

EEYORE: Don't mention it, Pooh.

POOH: Oh, Eeyore, I didn't mean that I didn't *want* to see you—

EEYORE: Quite—quite. But your new stripy friend—naturally, he wants his breakfast. What did you say his name was?

POOH: Tigger.

EEYORE: Then come this way, Tigger.

NARRATOR: Eeyore led the way to the most thistly-looking patch of thistles that ever was, and waved a hoof at it.

EEYORE: A little patch I was keeping for my birthday, but, after all, what are birthdays? Here today and gone tomorrow. Help yourself, Tigger.

NARRATOR: Tigger thanked him and looked a little anxiously at Pooh.

TIGGER: (whispering) Are these really thistles?

POOH: Yes.

TIGGER: What Tiggers like best?

POOH: That's right.

TIGGER: I see.

NARRATOR: So Tigger took a large mouthful, and he gave a large crunch.

TIGGER: *Ow!*

NARRATOR: Tigger sat down and put his paw in his mouth.

POOH: What's the matter?

EEYORE: Your friend appears to have bitten on a bee.

NARRATOR: Pooh's friend stopped shaking his head to get the prickles out, and explained that Tiggers didn't like thistles.

EEYORE: Then why bend a perfectly good one?

POOH: But you said, you *said* that Tiggers like everything except honey and haycorns.

TIGGER: (running round in circles with his tongue hanging out) *And* thistles.

POOH: (sadly) What are we going to do?

NARRATOR: Piglet knew the answer to that, and he said at once that they must go and see Christopher Robin.

EEYORE: You'll find him with Kanga.

NARRATOR: Eeyore came close to Pooh, and said in a loud whisper,

EEYORE: *Could* you ask your friend to do his exercises somewhere else? I shall be having lunch directly, and don't want it bounced on just before I begin. A trifling matter, and fussy of me, but we all have our little ways.

NARRATOR: Pooh nodded solemnly and called to Tigger,

POOH: Come along and we'll go and see Kanga. She's sure to have lots of breakfast for you.

NARRATOR: Tigger finished his last circle and came up to Pooh and Piglet.

TIGGER: (smiling) Hot! Come on!

NARRATOR: Pooh and Piglet walked slowly after him. And as they walked Piglet said nothing, because he couldn't think of anything, and Pooh said nothing, because he was thinking of a poem. And when he had thought of it he began,

POOH: "What shall we do about poor little Tigger?
If he never eats nothing he'll never get bigger.
He doesn't like honey and haycorns and thistles
Because of the taste and because of the bristles.
And all the good things which an animal likes
Have the wrong sort of swallow or too many spikes."

PIGLET: He's quite big enough anyhow.

POOH: He isn't *really* very big.

PIGLET: Well, he *seems* so.

NARRATOR: Pooh was thoughtful when he heard this, and then he murmured to himself,

POOH: "But whatever his weight in pounds, shillings, and ounces,
He always seems bigger because of his bounces."
And that's the whole poem. Do you like it, Piglet?

PIGLET: All except the shillings. I don't think they ought to be there.

POOH: (explaining) They wanted to come in after the pounds, so I let them. It is the best way to write poetry, letting things come.

PIGLET: Oh, I didn't know.

NARRATOR: Tigger had been bouncing in front of them all this time, turning round every now and then to ask,

TIGGER: Is this the way?

NARRATOR: And now at last they came in sight of Kanga's house, and there was Christopher Robin. Tigger rushed up to him.

CHRISTOPHER ROBIN: Oh, there you are, Tigger! I knew you'd be somewhere.

TIGGER: (importantly) I've been finding things in the forest. I've found a pooh and a piglet and an eeyore, but I can't find any breakfast.

NARRATOR: Pooh and Piglet came up and hugged Christopher Robin, and explained what had been happening.

185

POOH: Don't *you* know what Tiggers like?

CHRISTOPHER ROBIN: I expect if I thought very hard I should, but I *thought* Tigger knew.

TIGGER: I do. Everything there is in the world except honey and haycorns and—what were those hot things called?

POOH: Thistles.

TIGGER: Yes, and those.

CHRISTOPHER ROBIN: Oh, well then, Kanga can give you some breakfast.

NARRATOR: So they went into Kanga's house, and when Roo had said,

ROO: Hallo Pooh, hallo Piglet, hallo Tigger,

NARRATOR: they told Kanga what they wanted, and Kanga said very kindly,

KANGA: Well, you look in my cupboard, Tigger dear, and see what you'd like.

NARRATOR: Because Kanga knew at once that, however big Tigger seemed to be, he wanted as much kindness as Roo.

POOH: Shall I look too?

NARRATOR: For Pooh was feeling a little eleven o'clockish. And he found a small tin of condensed milk, and something seemed to tell him that Tiggers didn't like this, so he took it into a corner by itself, and went with it to see that nobody interrupted it. But the more Tigger put his nose into this and his paw into that, the more things he found which Tiggers didn't like. And when he had found everything in the cupboard, and couldn't eat any of it, he said to Kanga,

TIGGER: What happens now?

NARRATOR: But Kanga and Christopher Robin and Piglet were all standing round Roo, watching him have his Extract of Malt. And Roo was saying,

ROO: Must I?

KANGA: Now, Roo dear, you remember what you promised.

TIGGER: (whispering to Piglet) What is it?

PIGLET: His Strengthening Medicine. He hates it.

NARRATOR: So Tigger came closer, and he leaned over the back of Roo's chair, and suddenly he put out his tongue, and took one large golollop, and, with a sudden jump of surprise, Kanga said,

KANGA: Oh!

NARRATOR: And Kanga clutched at the spoon again just as it was disappearing, and pulled it safely back out of Tigger's mouth. But the Extract of Malt was gone.

KANGA: Tigger *dear!*

ROO: (singing happily) He's taken my medicine, he's taken my medicine, he's taken my medicine!

NARRATOR: Then Tigger looked up at the ceiling, and closed his eyes, and his tongue went round and round his chops, in case he had left any outside, and a peaceful smile came over his face as he said,

TIGGER: So *that's* what Tiggers like!

NARRATOR: Which explains why he always lived at Kanga's house afterwards, and had Extract of Malt for breakfast, dinner, and tea. And sometimes, when Kanga thought he wanted strengthening, he had a spoonful or two of Roo's breakfast after meals as medicine.

PIGLET: But *I* think that he's been strengthened quite enough!

NARRATOR: The End.

ADMIT ONE

IN WHICH TIGGER COMES TO
THE FOREST AND HAS BREAKFAST

HONEY

At the Airport

from *Switcharound*

BY LOIS LOWRY

AT THE AIRPORT

Lois Lowry has written some very funny books. She wrote an entire series about Anastasia Krupnik and several other books that feature Caroline and J.P., the main characters from *Switcharound*. She has also written some serious novels, including *A Summer to Die* and *Autumn Street*.

When *Switcharound* begins, Caroline and J.P., who live with their mother in New York City, have just learned that they are to spend the summer in Des Moines, Iowa, with their father and his new family.

Neither Caroline nor J.P. is very happy with the prospect of a summer spent away from home. To make matters worse, they have been sworn enemies for as long as they can remember, and neither wants to spend three months stuck in a strange house with the other. Fortunately the summer has quite a few surprises in store for both Caroline and J.P.!

"At the Airport" provides a brief but funny introduction to a book you will certainly enjoy.

Players: 5

Narrator 1	J.P.	Caroline
Narrator 2		Mother

NARRATOR 1: I'm _____.
   I help tell the story.

NARRATOR 2: I'm _____.
   I also help tell the story.

J.P.: I'm _____.
   I play J.P.

CAROLINE: I'm _____.
       I play Caroline.

MOTHER: I'm _____.
       I play Caroline and J.P.'s mother.

NARRATOR 1:   We would like to present a section from *Switch-around* by Lois Lowry.

NARRATOR 2:   As our story begins, Caroline, J.P., and their mother have just arrived at the airport. Soon Caroline and J.P. will board the airplane that will take them to Des Moines to visit their father for the summer.

NARRATOR 1:   J.P. and Caroline are not always the best of friends.

J.P.:   Pretend you don't know me. I want to walk by myself. I don't want people to know I'm with you guys. Especially with *her* (gestures towards his sister).

CAROLINE: Jerk.

MOTHER: (frowning) James, walk by yourself if you want to. But keep us in sight, okay? This is a huge airport, and I don't want to lose you. The flight is number eight-nine-two, and it leaves at one-thirty from Gate 45. Do you both have everything? The stubs for the checked luggage are stapled to your tickets. Do you both have your tickets?

NARRATOR 1:   Caroline opened her pocketbook and showed her ticket to her mother. J.P. was looking the other way, pretending he'd never seen them before in his life. But

191

his ticket was visible, the end of it appearing at his jacket pocket.

MOTHER: Are you sure you don't want to check that bag? It looks heavy.

J.P.:   (muttering) I told you, it's my valuable stuff.

NARRATOR 2:   He shifted the small suitcase from one hand to the other. It made a clacking noise.

CAROLINE: It's all his tools, plus a dumb broken radio and a busted clock that he found in a trash can on Eighty-second Street.

J.P.:   (sarcastically) Why don't you print up announcements about my personal life, Caroline? Maybe you could stand on a street corner and distribute them.

MOTHER: I hope you two will outgrow this warfare. (looking at her watch) Okay. Onward. James, from now on we'll pretend we don't know you. But don't you *dare* wander off and get lost.

NARRATOR 1:   J.P. had shifted his clanking suitcase again and started off. Caroline walked behind him, with her mother.

NARRATOR 2:   Around them, crowds moved toward various gates and stairs and doors.

NARRATOR 1:   Caroline and her mother watched as J.P. stopped in front of a machine, set his clanking suitcase down and reached into his pocket for some change.

192

CAROLINE: (whispering to her mother) He's buying *cigarettes*!

MOTHER: (chuckling) No, he's not. It's a candy machine. Don't stare at him, Caroline. He hates that. Come on—we'll walk ahead, as if we don't know him.

NARRATOR 2:   At the entrance to the departure gates, Caroline and her mother put their pocketbooks onto the moving belt of the x-ray machine and walked through the metal detector. Caroline looked back and saw J.P. waiting in line to go through the security devices. He was munching on a candy bar.

CAROLINE: (reassuring her mother) He's still there. He didn't get lost.

NARRATOR 1:   Caroline and her mother reached Gate 45.

MOTHER: Now, your boarding pass is with your ticket. And I hate to tell you this, but you and your brother are sitting next to each other.

CAROLINE: (suspiciously) Who gets the window?

MOTHER: I can't remember which one has the window seat. But you can switch halfway there, to make it fair. Where *is* J.P.? I thought he was right behind us.

CAROLINE: (grabbing her mother's arm) Listen, they said your name.

NARRATOR 2:   They listened. Sure enough, the public address system was saying in its monotonous voice, "Joanna Tate. Please report to the security checkpoint."

NARRATOR 1:   Caroline and her mother hurried back to the place where they had last seen J.P. waiting in line. And there he still was. But he was surrounded by a cluster of uniformed airport officials.

NARRATOR 2:   His pockets were turned inside out, and the contents—

NARRATOR 1:   a jackknife

NARRATOR 2:   some small screwdrivers

NARRATOR 1:   and a pair of needlenose pliers were in front of him on a tray. They were the things J.P. always carried in his pocket.

NARRATOR 2:   In front of him, on a table, his small suitcase was open. Two men were examining the contents, and their faces were grim.

NARRATOR 1:   Carefully they removed the broken alarm clock that J.P. had retrieved from a trash can. Then they took out the radio with the missing dials.

NARRATOR 2:   One man poked suspiciously at the tangle of wires which protruded from a pocket of the suitcase.

MOTHER: (in a worried voice) What's the trouble?

J.P.:   (happily) Mom! That's my mom and my sister.

CAROLINE: (loudly) Gentlemen, we have never seen this person before in our lives!

NARRATOR 1: The End.

There's a Hole in My Bucket

Readers: 2

READERS 1 AND 2:   "There's a Hole in My Bucket"

READER 1:   There's a hole in my bucket, dear Henry, dear Henry.

READER 2:   Then mend it, dear Mabel, dear Mabel, please do.

READER 1:   With what shall I mend it, dear Henry, dear Henry?

READER 2:   With straw, my dear Mabel, dear Mabel, please do.

READER 1:   But the straw is too lo-ong, dear Henry, dear Henry.

READER 2:   Then trim it, dear Mabel, dear Mabel, please do.

READER 1:   But the knife is too blu-unt, dear Henry, dear Henry.

READER 2:   Then sharpen it, dear Mabel, dear Mabel, please do.

READER 1:   But the stone is too dry-y, dear Henry, dear Henry.

READER 2:   Then wet it, dear Mabel, dear Mabel, please do.

READER 1:   But how shall I wet it, dear Henry, dear Henry?

READER 2:   With water, dear Mabel, dear Mabel, with water.

READER 1:   How shall I fetch water, dear Henry, dear Henry?

READER 2:   Use the bucket, dear Mabel, dear Mabel, please do.

READER 1:   There's a hole in my bucket, dear Henry, dear Henry.

READER 2:   Then LEAVE IT, dear Mabel, dear Mabel, LEAVE IT.

I'm Tipingee, She's Tipingee, We're Tipingee, Too

from *The Magic Orange Tree*

BY DIANE WOLKSTEIN

I'M TIPINGEE, SHE'S TIPINGEE, WE'RE TIPINGEE, TOO

"I'm Tipingee, She's Tipingee, We're Tipingee, Too" is a tale that Diane Wolkstein, storyteller and folklorist, learned in Haiti and brought home to include in her collection of Haitian folktales, *The Magic Orange Tree*. It is the perfect Reader's Theater choice if you wish to try a play with lots of movement, for it contains more action than most of the selections.

Don't be dismayed by the portrayal of the stepmother. The stepmother as an evil stranger is a familiar motif in traditional folklore.

Tipingee is pronounced Te-PING-gee, with the emphasis on the middle syllable and the second "g" given a hard pronunciation, as in "geese." The three girls might like to practice their chant before you begin, so that the chorus will sound well coordinated.

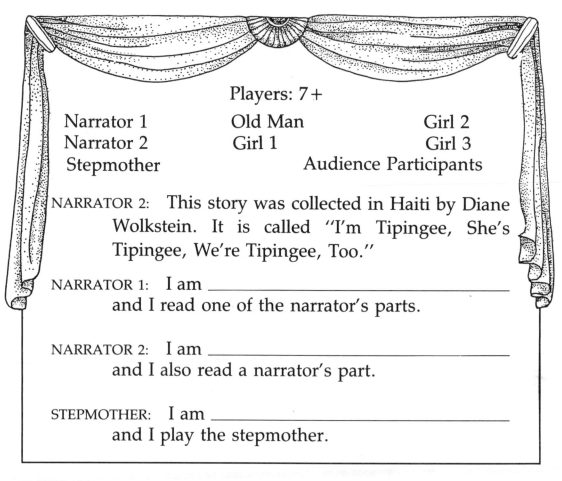

Players: 7+

Narrator 1	Old Man	Girl 2
Narrator 2	Girl 1	Girl 3
Stepmother		Audience Participants

NARRATOR 2: This story was collected in Haiti by Diane Wolkstein. It is called "I'm Tipingee, She's Tipingee, We're Tipingee, Too."

NARRATOR 1: I am _____
and I read one of the narrator's parts.

NARRATOR 2: I am _____
and I also read a narrator's part.

STEPMOTHER: I am _____
and I play the stepmother.

OLD MAN: I am _____
        and I play an old man.

GIRL 1:   I am _____
        and I play one of the girls.

GIRL 2:   I am _____
        and I play one of the girls.

GIRL 3:   I am _____
        and I too play one of the girls.

NARRATOR 1:   There was once a girl named Tipingee. Her stepmother was a selfish woman who didn't like to share her earnings with the girl.

NARRATOR 2:   One day the stepmother needed wood for the fire. She went into the forest to look for firewood. She stood in the middle of the forest and cried out,

STEPMOTHER: My friends, there is so much wood here and at home I have no wood. Who will help me carry the firewood?

NARRATOR 1:   Suddenly, an old man appeared.

OLD MAN: I will help you to carry the firewood. But then what will you give me?

STEPMOTHER: I have very little, but I will find something to give you when we get to my house.

NARRATOR 2:   The old man carried the firewood home for the stepmother.

199

OLD MAN: I have carried the firewood for you. Now what will you give me?

STEPMOTHER: I will give you a servant girl. I will give you my stepdaughter, Tipingee.

NARRATOR 1:   Now Tipingee was in the house, and when she heard her name she ran to the door and listened.

STEPMOTHER: Tomorrow I will send my stepdaughter to the well for water at noon. She will be wearing a red dress. Call her by her name, Tipingee, and she will come to you. Then you can take her.

OLD MAN: Very well. I will do that.

NARRATOR 2:   The old man went away.

NARRATOR 1:   Tipingee ran to her friends. She ran to the houses of all the girls in her class at school and asked them to wear red dresses the next day.

NARRATOR 2:   At noon the next day the old man went to the well. He saw one little girl dressed in red. He saw a second little girl dressed in red. He saw a third little girl dressed in red.

OLD MAN: Which of you is Tipingee?

GIRL 1:   I'm Tipingee.

GIRL 2:   She's Tipingee.

GIRL 3:   We're Tipingee, too.

OLD MAN: Which of you is Tipingee?

NARRATOR 1:   The little girls began to clap and jump up and down and chant,

GIRL 1:   I'm Tipingee

GIRL 2:   She's Tipingee

GIRL 3:   We're Tipingee, too.

GIRL 1, GIRL 2, AND GIRL 3:   (clapping and jumping up and down)
I'm Tipingee
She's Tipingee
We're Tipingee, too.

NARRATOR 2:   The old man went to the woman.

OLD MAN: You tricked me. All the girls were dressed in red and each one said she was Tipingee.

STEPMOTHER: That is impossible. Tomorrow she will wear a black dress. Then you will find her. The one wearing a black dress will be Tipingee. Call her and take her.

NARRATOR 1:   But Tipingee heard what her stepmother said and ran and begged all her friends to wear black dresses the next day.

NARRATOR 2:   When the old man went to the well the next day, he saw one little girl dressed in black. He saw a second little girl dressed in black. He saw a third girl in black.

OLD MAN: Which of you is Tipingee?

201

GIRL 1: I'm Tipingee.

GIRL 2: She's Tipingee.

GIRL 3: We're Tipingee, too.

OLD MAN: Which of you is Tipingee?

NARRATOR 1: The girls joined hands and skipped about and sang,

GIRL 1: I'm Tipingee

GIRL 2: She's Tipingee

GIRL 3: We're Tipingee, too.

GIRL 1, GIRL 2, AND GIRL 3: (join hands and begin skipping)
I'm Tipingee
She's Tipingee
We're Tipingee, too.

NARRATOR 2: The man was getting angry. He went to the stepmother.

OLD MAN: You promised to pay me and you are only giving me problems. You tell me Tipingee but everyone here is Tipingee, Tipingee, Tipingee, Tipingee. If this happens a third time, I will come and take you for my servant.

STEPMOTHER: My dear sir, tomorrow she will be in red, completely in red. Call her and take her.

NARRATOR 1: And again Tipingee ran and told her friends to dress in red.

202

NARRATOR 2:   At noon the next day, the old man arrived at the well. He saw one little girl dressed in red. He saw a second little girl dressed in red. He saw a third girl in red.

OLD MAN: Which of you is Tipingee?

GIRL 1:   I'm Tipingee.

GIRL 2:   She's Tipingee.

GIRL 3:   We're Tipingee, too.

OLD MAN: (shouting) WHICH OF YOU IS TIPINGEE?

NARRATOR 1:   But the girls just clapped and jumped up and down and sang (speaking to the audience, say Help us with the chant),

GIRL 1:   I'm Tipingee

GIRL 2:   She's Tipingee

GIRL 3:   We're Tipingee, too.

GIRL 1, GIRL 2, AND GIRL 3:   (begin clapping and jumping up and down)
I'm Tipingee
She's Tipingee
We're Tipingee, too.

NARRATOR 2:   The old man knew he would never find Tipingee. He went to the stepmother and took her away. When Tipingee returned home, she was gone. So she lived in her own house with all her father's belongings. She was happy and she sang,

203

EVERYONE: I'm Tipingee
        She's Tipingee
        We're Tipingee, too.

        I'm Tipingee
        She's Tipingee
        We're Tipingee, too.
        The End.

Running the Gauntlet

by Kathleen Fraser

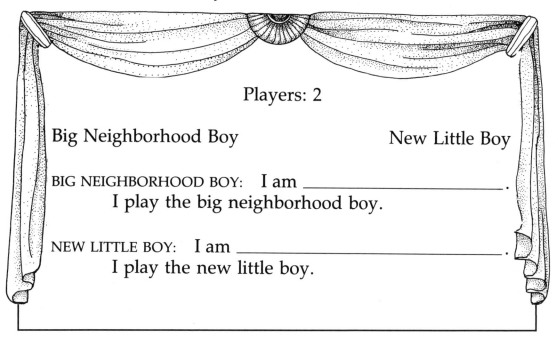

Players: 2

Big Neighborhood Boy   New Little Boy

BIG NEIGHBORHOOD BOY: I am _____.
     I play the big neighborhood boy.

NEW LITTLE BOY: I am _____.
     I play the new little boy.

BIG NEIGHBORHOOD BOY: Want to run the gauntlet?

NEW LITTLE BOY: How do you play?

BIG NEIGHBORHOOD BOY: Well, *we* all sit in a row on the grass, across from each other, and *you* have to run through our feet from one end of the row to the other.

NEW LITTLE BOY: Through all your knees and all your boots?

BIG NEIGHBORHOOD BOY: Yep.

NEW LITTLE BOY: Will you kick and bump? Will you trip me?

BIG NEIGHBORHOOD BOY: Well, sort of . . .

NEW LITTLE BOY: Will it hurt?

BIG NEIGHBORHOOD BOY: Not if you cross your eyes and wiggle your ears and run as fast as a lizard.

NEW LITTLE BOY: I think I'll just watch for a while.

The Thursday Call

from *Cracker Jackson*

BY BETSY BYARS

THE THURSDAY CALL

Betsy Byars has written more than twenty books for children. In *Cracker Jackson* she explores the subject of wife abuse through the eyes of a child. It is a combination of humorous and serious writing. This excerpt is an introduction to an excellent piece of children's literature.

Players: 5

Narrator 1   Jackson   Mom
Narrator 2   Dad

NARRATOR 1:   "The Thursday Call" from *Cracker Jackson* by Betsy Byars. I am _____. I read the part of a narrator.

NARRATOR 2:   I am _____. I also play a narrator.

JACKSON: I am _____. I play Cracker Jackson.

MOM: I am _____. I play Cracker Jackson's mom.

DAD: I am _____. I play Cracker Jackson's dad.

NARRATOR 2:   Cracker Jackson has a very important concern to discuss with his father.

JACKSON: Did Dad call?

MOTHER: No. You're out of breath, Jackson.

JACKSON: I know.

MOTHER: It's not good to ride so fast. When I told you to be home before dark, I didn't mean for you to—

JACKSON: I wasn't.

NARRATOR 1: He went into his mother's room and lay down on the bed to wait for his father's telephone call. Since his parents got divorced three years ago and his dad moved to L.A., his dad had called Jackson every Thursday night at exactly nine o'clock. He had never once missed calling, and Jackson had never once missed picking up the phone on the first ring.

NARRATOR 2: To his friends, Jackson pretended not to know the reason for his parents' divorce. If he had told them the real reason, they would not have believed him. Jackson's mother had divorced his father because he would not ever, under any circumstances, be serious.

NARRATOR 1: Like, if Jackson's mom said something like

MOTHER: Don't wipe your nose on your clothes, Jackson

NARRATOR 2: his dad would say

DAD: That's right, Jackson, wipe it on somebody else's clothes,

NARRATOR 2: and he would grab a perfect stranger's coat sleeve and say

209

DAD: Here you go, Son.

NARRATOR 1:   Even when something was serious—like the time his mom heard a rumor that Eastern was going to lay off a hundred stewardesses. His mom was very upset. She was crying.

MOM: I don't want to get another job. I love what I do. Flying means everything to me.

NARRATOR 2:   And Jackson's dad started pretending to be John Wayne. He said

DAD: If—flying—means—that—much—to—you,—Little—Lady—

NARRATOR 2:   He sounded more like John Wayne than John Wayne.

DAD: then—you'd— better—start—learning—to—flap—your—arms.

NARRATOR 1:   Jackson's earliest memory of his dad was of his not being serious.

NARRATOR 2:   He and his father were sitting on the sofa. His father was reading "The Three Bears," only he wouldn't read it right. He didn't have the Mama Bear say, "Somebody's been eating my porridge." He had her say

DAD: Somebody's been eating my low-fat yogurt.

JACKSON: No! Porridge!

NARRATOR 1:   He must have been up on this story because he was as upset as if his dad were taking liberties with the

Bible. He grabbed his dad's lips and tried to force them to say "porridge."

NARRATOR 2: His dad was laughing too hard.

DAD: Por—por—(laughing) por—por *porridge*!

NARRATOR 1: Jackson released his lips, but he sat up straight at his side, as alert as a soldier.

DAD: So, the Papa Bear says, "Somebody's been sleeping on my bed," and the Mama Bear says, "Somebody's been sleeping on my Serta Perfect-Sleeper," and the . . .

JACKSON: No! Bed! Say *bed*!

DAD: B—b—b (more laughter) give me a chance! I'll say it! I'll say it! I promise. Let my lips go. *Bed*!

NARRATOR 2: And so it went. One of the reasons Jackson got bored during reading at school was that the teachers read correctly. His father never read a story right in his life.

DAD: I think I can, but I'm not motivated. I think I can, but I'm not . . . Rapunzel, Rapunzel, let down your Miss Clairol–treated . . . Gretel, peep into my microwave . . . And I'll huff and I'll puff and I'll blow your double-wide, color-coordinated mobile home down . . . Who will help me eat the vitamin-enriched sourdough from Francisca?

NARRATOR 1: The phone rang, and Jackson picked it up. A voice said,

DAD: This is the President speaking to you from the Oval Office. Tonight I'd like to talk to you about a matter of concern to all Americans—aardvarks.

211

JACKSON: Hi, Dad.

DAD: How did you know it was me?

JACKSON: I already talked to the President tonight.

DAD: I should have known. So, how's it going?

JACKSON: All right.

DAD: How's school?

JACKSON: Fine.

DAD: You and Goat behaving yourselves?

JACKSON: No.

DAD: That's good. I don't want any son of mine behaving himself.

NARRATOR 1: He began to sound like Dracula.

DAD: There are vays to keep people from behaving themselves, and I vill use these vays if necessary.

NARRATOR 1: He laughed and then went back to his own voice.

DAD: So, what have you been up to?

JACKSON: Nothing. Oh, one thing happened. Do you remember a baby-sitter I had named Alma?

DAD: Not that big Swedish woman who didn't like me? Misterr Unterrr, git out off my kitchinn beforre I hit you overrr the head with the skilllet.

212

JACKSON: No, that was Anna. Alma was my summer baby-sitter for four years.

DAD: I remember Alma.

NARRATOR 2:   His voice got slow, Southern.

DAD: Jackson, why you sweet-potato casserole, you little gum-drop, you sugar-coated corn pone, you—

NARRATOR 2:   He sounded enough like Alma to make Jackson interrupt sharply.

JACKSON: Don't do that.

DAD: What?

JACKSON: Imitate Alma.

DAD: Why not? You let me imitate the President, the Queen of England, Mr. Rogers.

JACKSON: That's different.

DAD: How?

JACKSON: Alma's in trouble.

DAD: What kind of trouble?

JACKSON: I don't know exactly. I think her husband's beating her up.

NARRATOR 1:   Now that he had spoken the terrible words at last, his worries began to pour out. He could not have stopped himself if he tried.

JACKSON: I saw her in McDonald's last week and she had a black eye, and I was over at her house the week before and caught her putting ice on her lip. It was swollen bad. And tonight I went over there and—

DAD: You went to her house?

JACKSON: Yes, and her eye was still black and today she sent me a letter saying to keep away or he'd hurt me and—

DAD: What are you doing going to her house? If he's beating his wife, he's not going to hesitate about hitting you. Let me talk to your mother.

NARRATOR 2: For the first time in Jackson's memory, his father sounded serious.

JACKSON: (yelling) Dad, wait a minute. Listen—

DAD: I want to speak to your mother. Does she know about this?

JACKSON: No, I promised Alma I wouldn't tell her. Alma doesn't want Mom to know.

DAD: Let me speak to your mother.

NARRATOR 1: Jackson glanced up. His mother was standing in the doorway, looking concerned. She had heard him yelling at his father, something he had never done before in all their hundreds of phone calls.

NARRATOR 2: He put his hand over the phone.

JACKSON: Nothing's wrong, Mom. Go back in the living room.

214

NARRATOR 2:   It was an unwritten rule that he got to have private talks with his father.

MOTHER: Let me speak to your father.

JACKSON: Mom, this is my call!

NARRATOR 1:   On the phone his father was yelling.

DAD: Jackson, I want to speak to your mother. Call your mother to the phone this instant!

NARRATOR 2:   His mother and father were closing the gap, drawing together for strength like strangers with a common trouble. His mother came into the room. She held out her hand.

NARRATOR 1:   Jackson hesitated, and sighed. Shoulders sagging, he handed her the phone.

NARRATOR 2:   The End.

ADMIT ONE

THE THURSDAY CALL

The Common Egret

by Paul Fleischman

Readers: 2

READER 1: The Common Egret

READER 2: by Paul Fleischman

READER 1	READER 2:
	They call us
common	common
	egrets.
Common!	
	The injustice!
As if to be so white that	
snow	snow
	is filled with envy
clouds	clouds
	consumed with spite
that milk	that milk
	should seem molasses
rates as ordinary.	
Gold	Gold
should be so slandered	
diamonds	diamonds
scorned as worthless	
rubies	rubies
spurned	
	if common
egrets	egrets
	are but
common.	*common.*

216

Fooling the King

FOOLING THE KING

Of course this is silly, but it shows how a sensible little girl can fool a king, when all the wisemen have failed. This might be a good warm-up exercise preparation for more serious efforts, since the audience plays an important part and will enjoy participating. In fact, the narrator, as leader of the skit, should be aware that she or he may have to control the audience, which may want to participate too much!

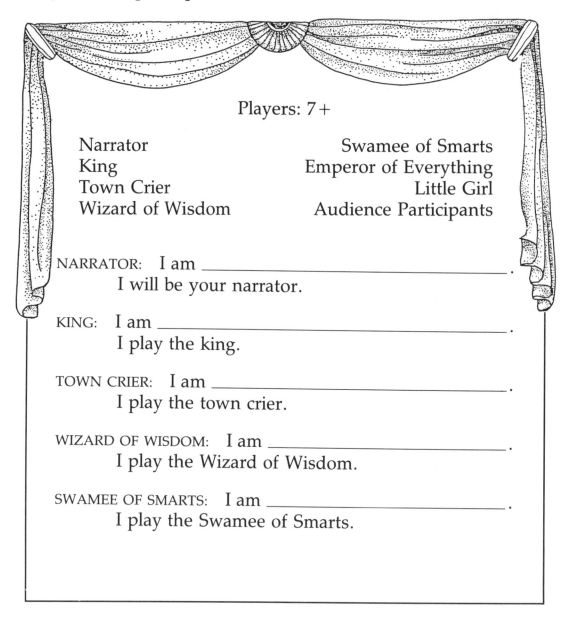

Players: 7+

Narrator   Swamee of Smarts
King   Emperor of Everything
Town Crier   Little Girl
Wizard of Wisdom   Audience Participants

NARRATOR: I am _____.
    I will be your narrator.

KING: I am _____.
    I play the king.

TOWN CRIER: I am _____.
    I play the town crier.

WIZARD OF WISDOM: I am _____.
    I play the Wizard of Wisdom.

SWAMEE OF SMARTS: I am _____.
    I play the Swamee of Smarts.

EMPEROR OF EVERYTHING: I am _____.
   I play the Emperor of Everything.

LITTLE GIRL: I am _____.
   I play the little girl.

NARRATOR: The king was bored.

KING: I'm very bored. I love jokes and riddles but I've heard
   them all.

NARRATOR: The king sent out a proclamation.

TOWN CRIER: Hear Ye! Hear Ye! Anyone who can fool the king
   will win a bag of gold.

NARRATOR: People came from far and wide to try to earn the bag
   of gold.

TOWN CRIER: The Wizard of Wisdom has come to ask you a
   riddle, sire.

KING: (bored) Go ahead. What's the riddle?

WIZARD OF WISDOM: How can you make pants last?

KING: Easy. You may make pants last if you make the coat and
   vest first.

NARRATOR: A little laughter please. (raise hand for audience to
   laugh and demonstrate false laughter: "Hee hee hee.")
   More please.

KING: (pointing at audience) Go ahead and laugh. I used to think that joke was funny. Now I'm just bored.

TOWN CRIER: The Swamee of Smarts has arrived to fool you, sire.

KING: (bored) Go ahead. What's the joke?

SWAMEE OF SMARTS: Why do hummingbirds hum?

KING: (bored) I know that one. Hummingbirds hum because they don't know the *words* to the songs.

NARRATOR: Audience, we need you once again. A little laughter, please. (raise and lower hand for laughter)

KING: Go ahead. Laugh. Your king is bored, bored, BORED.

TOWN CRIER: The Emperor of Everything has arrived to fool you, sire.

KING: (bored) Go ahead. What's the joke?

EMPEROR OF EVERYTHING: What goes up and never comes down?

KING: (bored) I know that one. What goes up and never comes down? Your age.

NARRATOR: Audience, we need you more than ever now. A little laughter, please. (raise and lower hand for laughter)

KING: Go ahead. Laugh. Your king is still bored.

TOWN CRIER: The little girl from down the street is here, sire.

KING: How can you possibly fool me? You're only in grade school.

GIRL: I'm not here to fool you. I'm here to collect the five bags of gold you owe me.

KING: What gold? What are you talking about?

GIRL: I've come to collect five bags of gold you said I could have last week when I walked your dog.

KING: (puzzled) What dog? What gold? I don't remember!

GIRL: I fooled you! I fooled you! Now you owe me at least one bag of gold!

NARRATOR: The king was amazed that a little girl could fool him.

KING: Here is your bag of gold.

GIRL: Thank you.

KING: It cost me a lot of gold to sit around being bored. I think I'll go out and buy a dog.

TOWN CRIER: Hear Ye. Hear Ye. Who has a dog to sell the king?

NARRATOR: But that's another story. This one ends here.

ADMIT ONE

FOOLING THE KING

The Wozzit

by Jack Prelutsky

Readers: 9

READER 5:   "The Wozzit" by Jack Prelutsky

READER 1:   There's a wozzit in the closet
and it's making quite a mess.

READER 2:   It has eaten father's trousers,
it has eaten mother's dress

READER 3:   and it's making so much noise
as it gobbles down my toys,

READER 4:   there's a wozzit in the closet—
oh I'm certain . . . yes, oh yes!

READER 5:   There's a wozzit in the closet
and I don't know what to do.

READER 6:   It has swallowed sister's slippers,
it has chewed upon my shoe,

READER 7:   now it's having its dessert
for it's stuffing down my shirt,

READER 8:   there's a wozzit in the closet—
yes, oh yes, I know it's true!

READER 9:   And I also know I'll never never
open up that closet,

ALL: for I never never never
ever
want to meet that wozzit.

Dragons and Giants

BY ARNOLD LOBEL

DRAGONS AND GIANTS

This chapter from *Frog and Toad Together* is the perfect play for older children to present to a younger class. There is a lot of movement in the story, and it works well as a full-blown play with lots of action—stones rumbling, a snake hissing, and a big bird swooping down. Try it both ways: as a Reader's Theater piece for your class and as a full presentation to the younger grades. It is a great introduction to Lobel's work.

Players: 8+

Narrator   Snake
Toad   Stones (at least three)
Frog   Hawk

NARRATOR: I am _____
       I play the narrator.

TOAD: I am _____
       I play Toad.

FROG: I am _____
       I play Frog.

SNAKE: I am _____
       I play Snake.

STONES: We are ____, ____, and ____. We play the
       stones.

HAWK: I am _____
       I play Hawk.

NARRATOR: Frog and Toad were reading a book together.

TOAD: The people in this book are brave.

FROG: They fight dragons and giants and they are never afraid. I wonder if we are brave.

NARRATOR: Frog and Toad looked into a mirror.

FROG: We look brave.

TOAD: Yes, but are we?

NARRATOR: Frog and Toad went outside.

FROG: We can try to climb this mountain. That should tell us if we are brave.

NARRATOR: Frog went leaping over rocks, and Toad came puffing up behind him. They came to a dark cave. A big snake came out of the cave.

SNAKE: Hello, lunch.

NARRATOR: The snake opened his wide mouth. Frog and Toad jumped away. Toad was shaking.

TOAD: (shouting) I am not afraid!

NARRATOR: They climbed higher, and they heard a loud noise.

STONES: (make a noise that sounds like stones rumbling down a mountain)

NARRATOR: Many large stones were rolling down the mountain.

TOAD: It's an avalanche!

NARRATOR: Frog and Toad jumped away. Frog was trembling.

FROG: (shouting) I am not afraid!

NARRATOR: They came to the top of the mountain. The shadow of a hawk fell over them.

HAWK: (flaps wings and makes a hawk sound)

NARRATOR: Frog and Toad jumped under a rock. The hawk flew away.

FROG AND TOAD: (screaming) We are not afraid!

NARRATOR: Then they ran down the mountain very fast. They ran past the place where they saw the avalanche. (stones rumble) They ran past the place where they saw the snake. (snake hiss) They ran all the way to Toad's house.

TOAD: Frog, I am glad to have a brave friend like you.

NARRATOR: He jumped into the bed and pulled the covers over his head.

FROG: And I am happy to know a brave person like you, Toad.

NARRATOR: He jumped into the closet and shut the door. Toad stayed in bed, and Frog stayed in the closet. They stayed there for a long time, just feeling brave together. The End.

The Land of the Bumbley Boo

by Spike Milligan

Readers: 3

ALL: "The Land of the Bumbley Boo" by Spike Milligan

READER 1: In the Land of the Bumbley Boo
The people are red white and blue,
They never blow noses,
Or ever wear closes,
What a sensible thing to do!

READER 2: In the land of Bumbley Boo
You can buy lemon pie at the Zoo;
They give away Foxes
In little Pink Boxes
And Bottles of Dandylion Stew.

READER 3: In the Land of Bumbley Boo
You never see a Gnu,
But thousands of cats
Wearing trousers and hats
Made of Pumpkins and Pelican Glue!

ALL: Oh, the Bumbley Boo! the Bumbley Boo!
That's the place for me and you!
So hurry! Let's run!
The train leaves at one!
For the Land of Bumbley Boo!
The wonderful Bumbley Boo-Boo Boo
The wonderful Bumbley BOO!!!

The Greedy Man's Week

by Beatrice Schenk de Regniers

Readers: 2

READER 1:   "The Greedy Man's Week"

READER 2:   by Beatrice Schenk de Regniers

READER 1:   On Monday

READER 2:   he eats a big pot of spaghetti.

READER 1:   On Tuesday

READER 2:   he says he's not hungry, and yet he gobbles a steak as big as a table.

READER 1:   On Wednesday

READER 2:   he says he is really not able to do more than nibble one or two noodles, and then he eats oodles!

READER 1:   On Thursday

READER 2:   he's thirsty and drinks quite a lot.

READER 1:   On Friday

READER 2:   he says, "I simply can not eat more than a few of these bananas," and then he eats two hundred bananas.

READER 1:   On Saturday

READER 2:   the greedy man asks the baker to bake an enormous whipped cream chocolate cake.

READERS 1 AND 2:   On Sunday
he has a stomach-ache.

When the Sky Is Like Lace

from the book
BY ELINOR LANDER HORWITZ

WHEN THE SKY IS LIKE LACE

This excerpt from *When the Sky Is Like Lace*, a picture book written by Elinor Lander Horwitz and beautifully illustrated by Barbara Cooney, makes a lovely Reader's Theater piece for older children to present to a younger class or perhaps to a group of parents or senior citizens on a special occasion.

In one of the many workshops in which I tested these plays, one participant wrote on her evaluation sheet that she didn't know what "bimulous" meant. But bimulous, of course, is not in Webster's dictionary. Enjoy the poetic nonsense in this piece. It will tempt you to read the entire book.

Readers: 5

ALL: We would like to present parts of *When the Sky Is Like Lace* by Elinor Lander Horwitz.

READER 1: On a bimulous night, the sky is like lace.

READER 2: Do you know how it looks when it's bimulous and the sky is like lace?

READER 3: It doesn't happen often, but when it does—KA-BOOM!—and everything is strange-splendid and plum-purple.

READER 4: If you plan to go out on a bimulous night when the sky is like lace, here are some rules you must remember:

READER 3: Never talk to a rabbit or a kissing gourami.

READER 2: If your nose itches, don't scratch it.

READER 1: Wear nothing that is orange, not even underneath.

READER 5: And—if you have a lucky penny, put it in your pocket. Because, on bimulous nights when the sky is like lace and the otters are singing and the snails are sulking and the trees are dancing and the grass is like gooseberry jam, it's a good idea to be prepared. Because—you never know.

READER 1: The next thing to talk about is the eating. On nights when it's bimulous and the sky is like lace, the thing to eat is spaghetti with pineapple sauce.

READER 4: After the eating comes the singing.

READER 2: After the singing come the presents.

READER 3: On bimulous nights when the sky is like lace, everyone exchanges presents like

READER 5: three fireflies in a jar

READER 2: anything chartreuse

READER 4: honey

READER 1: kites

READER 2: home-made marshmallow fudge

READER 3: a bag of red marbles

READER 5: a coconut

READER 2: After eating, the singing, and the presents, on nights when it's bimulous and the sky is like lace, and after the trees have stopped dancing, you might want to

231

READER 1:   ride a camel bareback

READER 2:   juggle three peaches,

READER 3:   gather cornflowers

READER 4:   dig clams

READER 5:   shout and yell and hop up and down in the mud

READER 2:   pretend to be a helicopter

READER 1:   play dominoes

READER 3:   tickle an elephant—

READER 4:   Pick any two you like best.

READER 1:   The last bimulous night happened three weeks ago
Wednesday before Tuesday.

READER 2:   Did you hear the otters sing?

READER 4:   The wind was rather whistly that night.

READER 3:   Did you see the trees dance the eucalyptus?

READER 4:   There were plum-purple shadows on the bedroom
ceiling.

READER 5:   Did you see that the sky was like lace?

READER 4:   Or did you fall asleep and miss it?

READER 5:   You had better be prepared next time.

READER 1:   Here's what you should do.

READER 2:   Each night from now on look out the window at the man in the moon through a clean white handkerchief before you get to bed.

READER 5:   If he winks his left eye, that's the signal.

READER 4:   Start cooking spaghetti and plan to be up all night.

READER 1:   And please take care not to speak to a rabbit or a kissing gourami.

READER 2:   And if your nose itches, don't scratch it.

READER 3:   And be sure not to put on anything orange—not even underneath.

READER 5:   Because you don't want to miss a thing

READER 1:   when the otters are tuning their voices

READER 2:   and the snails are lining up two by two

READER 3:   and the trees are aslant at the midnight end of the garden

READER 4:   and the sky—the sky—OH, LOOK AT THE SKY!

ALL: It's going to be PERFECTLY BIMULOUS!

233

My Favorite Word

by Lucia and James L. Hymes, Jr.

Readers: 4

ALL: "My Favorite Word"

READER 1: There is one word—

READER 2: My favorite—

READER 3: The very, very best.

READER 4: It isn't No or Maybe,

ALL: It's Yes, Yes, Yes, YES!

READER 1: "Yes, yes, you may," and

READER 2: "Yes, of course," and

READER 3: "Yes, please help yourself."

READER 4: And when I want a piece of cake, "Why, yes. It's on the shelf."

READER 1: Some candy?

ALL: "Yes."

READER 2: A cookie?

ALL: "Yes."

READER 3: A movie?

ALL: "Yes, we'll go." I love it when they say my word: Yes, YES, YES! (Not No.)

The Last Story

THE LAST STORY

The endless story is a familiar motif in folklore. The most famous of these stories appears in *The Arabian Nights*. "The Last Story" is a particularly appealing version because it doesn't just fade off, but truly does offer an ending to the endless story.

This is an easy story for children to memorize and would be the perfect selection if you are looking for a short play to perform without scripts before a more formal audience. It would also be an excellent encore piece if you want to perform more than one play.

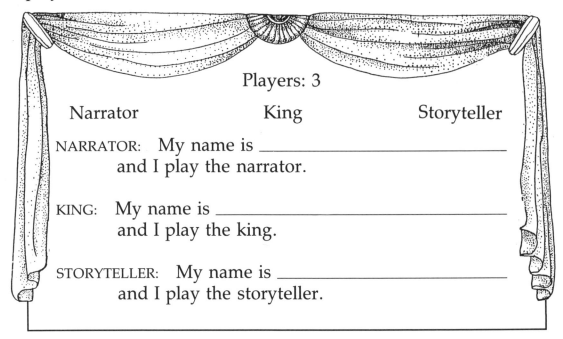

Players: 3

Narrator   King   Storyteller

NARRATOR: My name is _____
and I play the narrator.

KING: My name is _____
and I play the king.

STORYTELLER: My name is _____
and I play the storyteller.

NARRATOR: There was once a king who loved stories. He even had a storyteller who lived in his castle. It was the storyteller's job to entertain the king with stories any time of the day or night. One night the king could not sleep. He tossed and turned. At last he thought,

KING: Why should I stay up all night by myself? I need someone to entertain me. Storyteller, come here.

STORYTELLER: Yes, sire. What can I do for you?

KING: Tell me a story.

STORYTELLER: But sire, it is very late at night. I want to go to sleep.

NARRATOR: But the king replied,

KING: Tell me a story *now*.

NARRATOR: So, the storyteller began to tell the king a story.

STORYTELLER: Once upon a time there was a shepherd who was bringing his sheep to market. He had to bring his sheep from one side of the river to the other. He could only put one sheep in his little boat at a time. He had a lot of sheep, but he patiently put one sheep in the boat and rowed it across the river. Then he put another sheep in the boat and rowed it across the river. Then he put another sheep in the boat and rowed it across the river. Back and forth, back and forth, back and forth, back and forth, back and forth across the river the shepherd rowed his sheep.

KING: I'm a little bored with all these sheep. In fact, I'm getting sleepy.

STORYTELLER: I can understand that, sire. And unfortunately, the shepherd has several hundred more sheep to get across the river. Let me continue the story. And so the shepherd put another sheep into his boat and rowed it across the river, and then he put another sheep in the boat and rowed it across the river . . .

KING: But I'm very bored with all this rowing.

STORYTELLER: I'm sure that is so, Your Majesty. I have a suggestion. Since the shepherd has so many more sheep to row across the river, let's you and I go to sleep until all the sheep are safely across the river, and then we can continue the story.

KING: A very good idea.

NARRATOR: And so the king and the storyteller went to sleep. And a good thing too, because there are a lot more sheep on the shore waiting for the shepherd to row them across the river. Good night!